Designing for Human–Machine Symbiosis Using the URANOS Model:

Emerging Research and Opportunities

Benjamin Hadorn
University of Fribourg, Switzerland

A volume in the Advances in Human and Social Aspects of Technology (AHSAT) Book Series

www.igi-global.com

Published in the United States of America by
    IGI Global
    Information Science Reference (an imprint of IGI Global)
    701 E. Chocolate Avenue
    Hershey PA 17033
    Tel: 717-533-8845
    Fax: 717-533-8661
    E-mail: cust@igi-global.com
    Web site: http://www.igi-global.com

Library of Congress Cataloging-in-Publication Data

Names: Hadorn, Benjamin, 1978- author.
Title: Designing for human-machine symbiosis using the URANOS model :
  emerging research and opportunities / by Benjamin Hadorn.
Description: Hershey, PA : Information Science Reference, [2017] | Includes
  bibliographical references and index.
Identifiers: LCCN 2016050401| ISBN 9781522518884 (hardcover) | ISBN
  9781522518891 (ebook)
Subjects: LCSH: Human-machine systems--Design and construction. | Cooperating
  objects (Computer systems) | Ubiquitous computing.
Classification: LCC TA167 .H335 2017 | DDC 620.8/2--dc23 LC record available at https://lccn.
loc.gov/2016050401

This book is published in the IGI Global book series Advances in Human and Social Aspects of Technology (AHSAT) (ISSN: 2328-1316; eISSN: 2328-1324)

British Cataloguing in Publication Data
A Cataloguing in Publication record for this book is available from the British Library.

Advances in Human and Social Aspects of Technology (AHSAT) Book Series

ISSN:2328-1316
EISSN:2328-1324

Editor-in-Chief: Ashish Dwivedi, The University of Hull, UK

MISSION

In recent years, the societal impact of technology has been noted as we become increasingly more connected and are presented with more digital tools and devices. With the popularity of digital devices such as cell phones and tablets, it is crucial to consider the implications of our digital dependence and the presence of technology in our everyday lives.

The **Advances in Human and Social Aspects of Technology (AHSAT) Book Series** seeks to explore the ways in which society and human beings have been affected by technology and how the technological revolution has changed the way we conduct our lives as well as our behavior. The AHSAT book series aims to publish the most cutting-edge research on human behavior and interaction with technology and the ways in which the digital age is changing society.

COVERAGE

- Cyber Behavior
- Technology Adoption
- Cyber Bullying
- Technology Dependence
- Cultural Influence of ICTs
- Activism and ICTs
- Public Access to ICTs
- Human Development and Technology
- Human-Computer Interaction
- Digital Identity

IGI Global is currently accepting manuscripts for publication within this series. To submit a proposal for a volume in this series, please contact our Acquisition Editors at Acquisitions@igi-global.com or visit: http://www.igi-global.com/publish/.

Titles in this Series

For a list of additional titles in this series, please visit:
http://www.igi-global.com/book-series/advances-human-social-aspects-technology/37145

Solutions for High-Touch Communications in a High-Tech World
Michael A. Brown Sr. (Florida International University, USA)
Information Science Reference • ©2017 • 217pp • H/C (ISBN: 9781522518976) • US $185.00

Design Solutions for User-Centric Information Systems
Saqib Saeed (Imam Abdulrahman Alfaisal University, Saudi Arabia) Yasser A. Bamarouf (Imam Abdulrahman Alfaisal University, Saudi Arabia) T. Ramayah (University Sains Malaysia, Malaysia) and Sardar Zafar Iqbal (Imam Abdulrahman Alfaisal University, Saudi Arabia)
Information Science Reference • ©2017 • 422pp • H/C (ISBN: 9781522519447) • US $215.00

Identity, Sexuality, and Relationships among Emerging Adults in the Digital Age
Michelle F. Wright (Masaryk University, Czech Republic)
Information Science Reference • ©2017 • 343pp • H/C (ISBN: 9781522518563) • US $185.00

Enriching Urban Spaces with Ambient Computing, the Internet of Things, and Smart...
Shin'ichi Konomi (Univ. of Tokyo, Japan) and George Roussos (Univ. of London, UK)
Engineering Science Reference • ©2017 • 323pp • H/C (ISBN: 9781522508274) • US $210.00

Handbook of Research on Individualism and Identity in the Globalized Digital Age
F. Sigmund Topor (Keio University, Japan)
Information Science Reference • ©2017 • 645pp • H/C (ISBN: 9781522505228) • US $295.00

Information Technology Integration for Socio-Economic Development
Titus Tossy (Mzumbe University, Tanzania)
Information Science Reference • ©2017 • 385pp • H/C (ISBN: 9781522505396) • US $200.00

Handbook of Research on Human-Computer Interfaces, Developments, and Applications
João Rodrigues (University of Algarve, Portugal) Pedro Cardoso (University of Algarve, Portugal) Jânio Monteiro (University of Algarve, Portugal) and Mauro Figueiredo (University of Algarve, Portugal)
Information Science Reference • ©2016 • 663pp • H/C (ISBN: 9781522504351) • US $330.00

For an enitre list of titles in this series, please visit:
http://www.igi-global.com/book-series/advances-human-social-aspects-technology/37145

IGI GLOBAL
DISSEMINATOR OF KNOWLEDGE

www.igi-global.com

701 East Chocolate Avenue, Hershey, PA 17033, USA
Tel: 717-533-8845 x100 • Fax: 717-533-8661
E-Mail: cust@igi-global.com • www.igi-global.com

Table of Contents

Preface

Throughout the history of mankind, big efforts were undertaken to improve the prosperity, security and welfare of humanity and society. Technological progress contributed significantly to the evolutionary development of society. With each technological achievement, human beings as well as their socio-cultural and natural environments face new challenges and problems. As an example, recent efforts in pervasive and mobile computing lead to a dramatic networking of people, of their ideas, thoughts and feelings. Information can be quickly shared and used by communities to build knowledge, mainly for new developments and businesses. But, in addition to the benefits, there are also new challenges and limitations, such as the disappearance of privacy, the technological dependence or the feeling of being remotely observed and driven by possibly intelligent systems.

Nowadays, there is an increasing demand for integral and sustainable solutions to face these challenges. Many people feel a greater need to participate actively in the decision-making and control processes, rather than being dependent on technology or being controlled by intelligent systems. There is a need to emphasize our individual, social and cultural dimensions, and to resist against being handled through standardization lenses, and even against being rejected (pushed towards irrelevance). In this context, a holistic integration of humans into technical systems becomes increasingly important.

With the new approach proposed in this book, we try to integrate human beings and their natural, informational and socio-cultural environments into system design. This human-centered initiative is a movement towards integral and holistic development, which puts the human and his environment in the center of design and of activation processes. In this sense, this work contributes to paving a new way of defining reality, which allows research and engineering to proceed towards a more humanistic and sustainable construction of human-centered systems (HCSs).

This chapter starts by presenting our research goals in section "Research Goals". Section "Focus of the" introduces our research in more detail, particularly focusing on our approaches in generic and human-centered system modeling. In section "Research Challenges" major research challenges are addressed. The contributions of this book are summarized in section "Contributions". Assumptions about complex and non-linear systems are listed in section "Assumptions". And finally, section "Organization of the Book" outlines the rest of the book.

RESEARCH GOALS

This research pursues the goal of providing a generic and a human-centered system model addressing interactions in large scale, complex and non-linear systems, such as pervasive computing systems, smart environments and smart industrial machines. This general goal can be met through two sub-goals.

The first sub-goal is to develop a generic system model (cf. chapter "URANOS: A Generic System Model") which considers a system as a whole, including all relevant interacting entities equivalently but differently, be they human beings, devices, machines or even elements of the environment. That is, each entity should be modeled and integrated into a system depending on the entity's complexity. For instance, a human is handled as a holistic and social being. In chapter "Model Instantiations", the genericity and the universality of our model is verified and demonstrated in three concrete model instantiations, in the domains of computer science, of socio-biology and of integral thinking.

The second sub-goal of this research is to propose a comprehensive and humanistic model for the human-centered design initiative (cf. chapter "Towards Human-centered System Design"). A use case in computer science shows how humans and machines can collaborate with each other and enter into a symbiotic relationship. This contributes to cyber-physical system (CPS) research and pervasive computing, providing new ways to handle human beings within their models.

FOCUS OF THE BOOK

This book focuses on two aspects: (1) providing a generic system model describing complex and non-linear systems, in particular living systems; and (2) human-centered system modeling.

Generic Approach

A generic system model called URANOS is presented. It is a cybernetic and systemic model providing a comprehensive and holistic view on complex and non-linear systems. In this context, the term "epistemological standpoint" is used to describe a world view through which someone can attain and explain his knowledge. URANOS combines three epistemological standpoints and their corresponding realities, namely objectivism, subjectivism and holism into a wholeness. Each standpoint describes its entities on a corresponding modeling plane. This principle has its roots in the meta-physical model of E. Schwarz (2002).

Complex systems are described in URANOS by various systemic orders. The lowest systemic order describes a system from the standpoint of objectivity, for instance through physical or chemical formulations and models. In these models, the observer is considered as external and not as an integral part of the system. Second-order systems include the observer and his subjective perception. URANOS explicitly describes the dynamics of how objective and subjective realities mutually influence one another. Finally, the third-order system addresses holistic and social beings and their consciousness.

Our generic model describes how entities can collaborate with each other. In this context, collaboration is a complex interaction that happens on all levels, objective, subjective and holistic. URANOS describes collaboration by cybernetic feedback loops, which lead to a symbiotic relationship between the participating entities.

URANOS aims at encouraging interdisciplinary work and reinforces the understanding of complex systems in general. Therefore, it provides a comprehensive framework and terminology for researchers and engineers from different domains. In three specific model instantiations, we show how URANOS can be applied to other research domains. The first instantiation addresses human beings and their natural, informational and socio-cultural environment. In a second instantiation, a holistic model for integral thinking is presented based on the AQAL-model from K. Wilber (2007). And finally, a coordination model for cyber-physical and multi-agent systems is proposed, handling objective, subjective and cognitive coordination processes.

Human-Centered Approach

Human-centered approaches are characterized by design and operation processes, which focus on human beings and their natural and socio-cultural environments. Primarily, human-centeredness needs a rethinking and paradigm shift within the research and engineering disciplines. We argue that human-centeredness cannot solely be achieved through super intelligent computer systems mimicking human beings. As a central element, we propose the principle of conversation theory by G. Pask (1975). It allows human beings and machines to enter into a conversation process allowing them to exchange novel concepts, ideas, goals and intentions. Through this complex interaction, participants can learn from each other, which may lead to a mutual agreement of understanding. It allows to integrate human skills and values to make them accessible to technical systems, similarly to the way they are accessible to humans in human-to-human interaction. We show how conversation becomes an integral part of the human-centered design.

To illustrate our approach, a case study is presented. It describes a prototype design addressing a new generation of cyber-physical applications and human-centered machines for industries which operate in the context of the fourth industrial revolution (Kagermann, Wahlster & Helbig, 2013). The outstanding feature of these machines is that they can enter into a conversation with human beings, together forming an adaptive learning organization.

Limits

In this thesis, we considered only three model instantiations. Of course, they cannot be seen as a complete validation of our generic approach and more instantiations are needed in other research domains like economy or organizational sciences.

Our research mainly addresses human-centered system design from a theoretical and modeling perspective. As a case study, the focus was to develop a design prototype. The development of a real prototype for evaluation was not the focus. This will be a follow-up of our research work.

RESEARCH CHALLENGES

A challenge of this research was to show how human beings can be integrated into a system holistically and comprehensively, leading towards a human-centered system design. It was important to find the right concept to get a deeper understanding of how humans and machines interact with each other and can form a symbiosis through collaboration.

Holism is still rarely used in technical sciences, like computer science. It was challenging to follow a holistic and generic approach which is underpinned namely with the philosophical approaches of K. Wilber (1995) and E. Morin (1992). Very little of their work has already been established in the research community of computer science.

Another challenge was to develop a generic system model that can be usefully instantiated for different domains. Following holistic and integral approaches brought new aspects to light. Others still remain open, such as the mind-body problem.

CONTRIBUTIONS

This work provides a new way ot think about technology and design. Here, human beings and their environments are put first. It is a step towards integral development by making the epistemological standpoints of subjectivism and holism available for researchers and engineers.

The main contributions of our work are:

- The development of the generic system model URANOS, providing a terminology for complex and non-linear systems. It provides a deeper understanding of such systems, their dynamics, and collaborative and symbiotic behaviors.
- A holistic framework allowing to integrate different epistemological perspectives into one comprehensive system model. Where each one has its own space to express and model its aspects.
- A paradigm shift towards more human-centered and sustainable solutions reinforcing the notion of humans as holistic and social beings.
- The proposal of several design principles for human-centered design, which are derived from our generic and integral standpoint.
- A model for human-machine collaboration, which integrates humans and machines into a human-centered system.
- A prototype design usable for various cyber-physical applications, in particular in the industrial context.

Assumptions

In order to be consistent with the hypothesis of providing a generic system model, several aspects in our research work were assumed or taken for granted. This section comprises the most important assumptions, namely non-linear systems and system complexity.

Open and Non-Linear Systems

The human-centered approach is accompanied by the realization that every system is in an interaction with its environment. In this sense, we consider all systems as open systems, except the universe, which is considered by definition as closed. This means, that all parts and processes are somehow directly or indirectly connected to each other.

In this context, modeling an open system means using an approximation and accepting that some of the modeling parameters remain unknown. Some interactions with parts outside the modeling scope are omitted (consciously or unconsciously). One has to be aware that a model forms an artificial system boundary. This means, that the boundary depends on an observer's point of view, and that the model cannot be used for an exact prediction of the system's behavior.

The behavioral predictability is a main characteristic of systems. A system is referred to as non-linear, if a system's output is not directly proportional to its inputs. Mathematically, the system does not satisfy the properties of additivity and homogeneity. Such systems appear to have a chaotic, unpredictable or counterintuitive behavior.

System Complexity

System complexity means two things: first, the degree of interconnectedness between a system's components, and second, the degree of unpredictability. We prefer this view, since both measures can be objectively determined. There are other definitions, but they are partially based on subjective parameters such as the degree of comprehensibility (simple, complicated).

System complexity can be illustrated in a two-dimensional representation (Figure 1). The first dimension is the degree of interconnectedness, while the second dimension addresses the degree of unpredictability.

Complex systems are a combination of high connectivity and of non-linear behavior. New system properties emerge from this combination, which are not simply derivable from the properties of a system's components.

ORGANIZATION OF THE BOOK

The book starts with the focus on generic system modeling (Figure 2). Chapter "Generic System Models - Background and Related Work" presents the background and related work that influenced our research. The disciplines of

Figure 1. Spectrum of system complexity

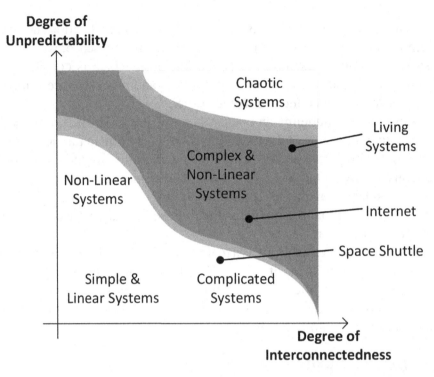

cybernetics, systemics and coordination are enlightened. In chapter "URANOS: A Generic System Model", our generic system model, called URANOS, is presented. It represents the core chapter of this book, addressing a modeling framework able to integrate epistemological standpoints, systemic orders, dynamics, and system development.

In chapter "Model Instantiations", URANOS is instantiated in three specific models. The first model describes human beings as holistic and spiritual beings, who are embedded in a physical, informational and socio-cultural environment. The second model deals with integral thinking and extends the AQAL-model of K. Wilber (2007) with system dynamics and an explicit holistic standpoint. Finally, a coordination model is presented which deals with objective, subjective and cognitive coordination processes. These three models build the core for human-centered systems.

Chapter "Towards Human-centered System Design" presents our model for human-centered system design. It starts with the state of the art of the human-centered initiative. Then, several design principles are proposed, which help designers and users to analyze, design and run human-centered systems. Based on them, a model for human-machine collaboration is derived,

Figure 2. Organization of the book

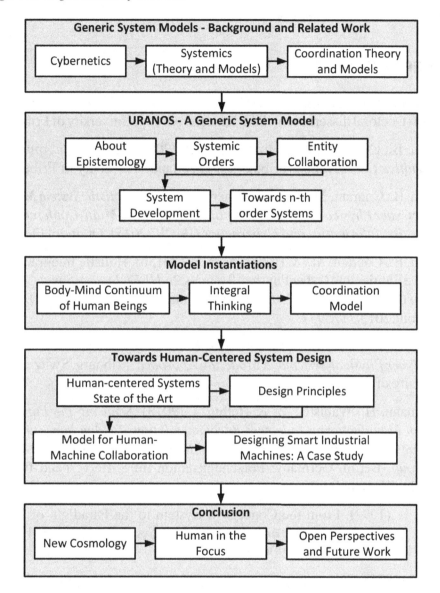

which holistically interconnects humans and machines with each other. The chapter ends with a case study applying this model to industrial machines.

Finally, the book ends with chapter "Conclusion" reviewing this work. It gives a glimpse of new perspectives and possible future research work.

The content of this book is based on the PhD thesis of B. Hadorn (2016c), and appears in part in publications by the author and co-author M. Courant and B. Hirsbrunner: Hadorn, Courant, and Hirsbrunner (2014a, 2015a, 2015b, 2016b).

Benjamin Hadorn
University of Fribourg, Switzerland

REFERENCES

Hadorn, B. (2016c). *URANOS - A Generic System Model for Human-Centered Design* (Doctoral dissertation). PAI-Research Group, University of Fribourg.

Hadorn, B., Courant, M., & Hirsbrunner, B. (2014a). *A Holistic Approach to Cognitive Coordination.* Fribourg, Switzerland: University of Fribourg.

Hadorn, B., Courant, M., & Hirsbrunner, B. (2015a). *Holistic System Modelling for Cyber Physical Systems. In The 6th International Multi-Conference on Complexity, Informatics and Cybernetics (IMCIC 2015).* Orlando, FL: IIIS.

Hadorn, B., Courant, M., & Hirsbrunner, B. (2015b). Holistic Integration of Enactive Entities into Cyber Physical Systems. *2nd IEEE International Conference on Cybernetics, CYBCONF 2015.* Gdynia, Poland: IEEE. doi:10.1109/CYBConf.2015.7175947

Hadorn, B., Courant, M., & Hirsbrunner, B. (2016b). *Towards Human-Centered Cyber Physical Systems: A Modeling Approach.* Fribourg, Switzerland: University of Fribourg.

Kagermann, H., Wahlster, W. & Helbig, J. (2013). *Securing the Future of German Manufacturing Industry: Recommendations for Implementing the Strategic Initiative INDUSTRIE 4.0, Final Report of the Industrie 4.0 Working Group.* Berlin, Germany: Forschungsunion im Stifterverband für die Deutsche Wirtschaft e.V.

Morin, E. (1992). From the Concept of System to the Paradigm of Complexity. *Journal of Social and Evolutionary Systems*, *15*(4), 371–385. doi:10.1016/1061-7361(92)90024-8

Pask, G. (1975). *Conversation, Cognition and Learning: A Cybernetic Theory and Methodology.* New York, NY: Elsevier Publishing Company.

Schwarz, E. (2002). Can Real Life Complex Systems Be Interpreted with the Usual Dualist Physicalist Epistemology - Or is a Holistic Approach Necessary? *Proceedings of the fifth European Systems Science Congress*, *2*, 1-9.

Wilber, K. (1995). *Sex, Ecology, Spirituality: The Spirit of Evolution*. Boston, MA: Shambhala Publications.

Wilber, K. (2007). *The Integral Vision: A Very Short Introduction to the Revolutionary Integral Approach to Life, God, the Universe, and Everything*. Boston, MA: Shambhala Publications.

Acknowledgment

Writing a PhD thesis is a long-term project in which many impressions are attained, and into which a lot of time and effort has been invested.

Writing about the experiences and knowledge at the end in this concentrated form, was a big challenge, one which would hardly have been possible without external support. First, I would like to thank Prof. Dr. Béat Hirsbrunner for his support of this work. Under his leadership and with his confidence in my work, it was possible to explore and develop these generic approaches. Furthermore, I would also like to thank Dr. Michèle Courant and Dr. Paul Pangaro for their valuable input into this project. They gave me deep insights into integral thinking and cybernetics. Special thanks also to Dr. Agnes Lisowska Masson. With her support and meticulous corrections, she helped me to improve my English.

A very special thanks goes to my family, my wife Manuela and my daughters Aylin and Elen. They often had to spend time without their husband and father in the last few years. Without their emotional support, this project would not have happened.

Benjamin Hadorn
University of Fribourg, Switzerland

Chapter 1
Generic System Models:
Background and Related Work

ABSTRACT

Systemic and holistic approaches provide a new way of thinking about, understanding and designing systems. In this chapter we aim to highlight the most significant and influential work in this trend, and in particular the achievements of cybernetics, systemics and coordination modeling. Starting with cybernetics, related topics like cybernetic orders, self-organization, autopoiesis and conversation theory are explained. Systemics, and especially general system theory, provide a general language and terminology to express and model systems independent of any research domain. Together with integral and system thinking, this leads to a paradigm shift in understanding and modeling complex and non-linear systems. Concretely, we introduce the meta model of Schwarz which was the starting point of our own generic system model URANOS. Finally, the coordination theories and models which had a great impact on our research on human-centered design are outlined.

INTRODUCTION

Our research is rooted in artificial intelligence, but also focuses on coordination, pervasive computing and human-computer interaction (HCI). In this context we mainly study coordination models, middleware design and pervasive technologies. Our latest research findings indicate that a paradigm shift is required, in particular for addressing human-machine interaction. We need to change our point of view, so that human beings can be holistically

DOI: 10.4018/978-1-5225-1888-4.ch001

integrated into our models and systems. This brings our research focus back to generic approaches, like cybernetics and general system theory.

The chapter starts with a section on "Cybernetics", an interdisciplinary research field, studying system governance and dynamics from a very generic point of view. Different approaches within cybernetics are central for URANOS, like first and second-order cybernetics, self-organizatio n, autopoiesis and conversation theory.

Some fundamental work in systemics, which is based on cybernetics, is presented in the section "Systemics." This work brought forth systems and integral thinking, which help to holistically conceive systems. Our model URANOS has its roots in this domain, especially in the meta physical model from E. Schwarz, explaining reality from different epistemological standpoints.

In the "Coordination" section evolutionary research on coordination is outlined. Coordination had a huge influence in developing URANOS, since URANOS is a continuation of our generic coordination model. In particular, the theories, models and languages most influencing for our work are presented. Finally, "Summary" section summarizes the background and related work on generic systems.

CYBERNETICS

Many research fields like mathematics, physics, computer science, biology and sociology face the challenge of modeling and analyzing complex and non-linear systems. Cybernetics, as an interdisciplinary approach, addresses this topic. The term "Cybernetics" originally comes from the Greek "κυβερνητικη" (kybernetike), meaning "governance" or "steersman". Cybernetics is primarily concerned with behavioral issues like goal directedness, functional behavior, complex decision-making and learning, rather than the structural organization of a system. It provides a generic framework in which systems (artificial or natural) can be ordered, related and understood (Ashby, 1957).

This section begins with the origin of cybernetics. Thereafter, two cybernetic orders are presented, followed by the principles of self-organization and autopoiesis. Finally, cybernetic conversation theory closes this section.

Origins

In the 1940's and 1950's the *Macy Conferences* (Pias, 2016) brought together post-war intellectuals from different research areas like electro- and mechanical-engineering, mathematical logic, biology, anthropology, psychology, linguistics and philosophy. The participants, among others W. McCulloch, M. Mead, N. Wiener, H. von Foerster, J. von Neumann and C.E. Shannon (C.E. Shannon participated in the conference as a guest), aimed to explore common principles expressed in their research domains. It became apparent that feedback and control loops exist in different research domains. In many cases, they cause endless recursion, which is regarded as very problematic.

Based on the Macy Conferences and his study of control and feedback loops, N. Wiener wrote his book *Cybernetics: or Control and Communication in the Animal and the Machine*, where he defined cybernetics as *"the scientific study of control and communication in the animal and the machine"* (Wiener, 1948). One of the major concerns in his book was feedback loops that can be found in human and animal reflexes as well as in technical systems. This led to his intention to develop a general theory describing organizational and control relations within systems, artificial or natural. The confluence of N. Wiener's work and the Macy Conferences was the birth of cybernetics.

The focus was originally on processes which occur either in machines or living systems. This also included cybernetic implications on cognitive and social systems, as addressed by N. Wiener (Wiener, 1950). Ever since, cybernetics has become an interdisciplinary study of complex systems and system dynamics in a very general sense. Even today, a small community of researchers studies this issue, but mostly cybernetics is nowadays an integral part of specific research disciplines, such as mechanical-engineering, artificial intelligence or sociology.

First-Order Cybernetics

In the early stage of cybernetics, systems are described as "things" that exist independently from any observer and his consciousness. Such models are based on well-bounded systems that can be observed from the outside. The observer is not part of the system. He observes and explores the internal relations between entities through purpose, teleology, control and feedback (Yolles & Fink, 2014).

This rather mechanical approach is called *first-order cybernetics*. It is based on the *objectivist positivist* point of view, where the observer's mind is supposed to discover the reality. As stated by K. Krippendorff (1986) *"first order cybernetics is concerned with circular causal processes e.g. control, negative feedback, computing, adaption"*. In this context, a process measures variables in an environment and compares them with a goal. Differences are attempted to be compensated for by appropriate actions. In this work, such feedback loops are referred to as "dampening feedback".

A mathematical control theory was developed from first-order cybernetics (Sontag, 1998). It considers the control of dynamic systems, in particular, how their behavior can be modified by dampening feedback. Here, a control process is divided into four functional steps (Figure 1):

1. Objects (quantities) in the environment are measured;
2. The obtained values are compared with a presetting;
3. A new output is calculated; and
4. The output is applied to the environment.

Control theory is applied in many engineering disciplines today, like mechanical engineering, medical technologies and aeronautics.

W.T. Powers et al. (2008) developed a theory of control that goes beyond simple steering of some variables in an environment. With the Perceptual Control Theory (PCT), they provided a conceptual framework than aimed to understand the phenomena of control, especially when biological organisms are involved. In PCT, perception is regarded as a dynamic function, which influences the adaptation and behavior of an organism. In this sense, adaptation and behavior cannot be treated independently from the perceived circumstances.

Second-Order Cybernetics

As several scientific domains like computer science and control engineering became independent of cybernetics in the 1960's and 1970's, they also took over the mechanistic approach of first-order cybernetics for modeling their systems. This circumstance still influences the way researchers and engineers in these disciplines proceed. For instance, in many engineering disciplines, operators and designers are considered to be external entities who observe, influence and control the system from the outside.

Figure 1. First-order cybernetics

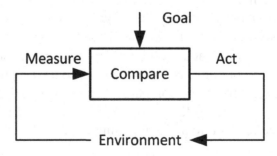

Cyberneticians realized that their original approach of first-order cybernetics had been too mechanistic for addressing social and living systems. Consequently, around the 1970's cybernetics took a significant step away from its previous mechanistic approach, emphasizing self-organization, autonomy, cognition and the assimilation of the observer. In this paradigm shift, the observer is included in a larger circularity where he enters into his own observation. The shift was heightened by insights from quantum mechanics, where the result of an observation always depends on the interaction between the observer and the observed entity. The study of this new approach became known as *second-order cybernetics* or *cybernetics of cybernetics* (von Foerster, 1992). Both the observer and the observed are cybernetic systems that depend on each other. Their interdependency and dynamics can be illustrated as a double loop. The inner loop (the observed system) is described by first-order cybernetics. The outer loop represents the observer. He observes the same environment as in the observed system, but his actions lead to changes in the inner loop's goals (Figure 2).

Second-order cybernetics has also been strongly influenced by the work of G. Pask, H.R. Maturana and F.J. Varela. From their constructivist and relativist perspectives, they argued that the internal structure and the system boundary (e.g. mental or physical) is generated through interactions forming an operationally closed system (Maturana, Varela & Beer, 1980).

Figure 2. Second-order cybernetics illustrated as a double loop

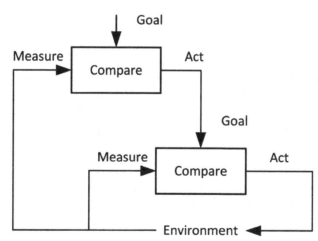

Self-Organization

Self-organization is one of the key features in complex and non-linear systems. It describes a form of system development, whereby the entropy decreases within a system, without being coordinated or managed externally.

W.R. Ashby brought the term "self-organization" to system science and cybernetics. His goal was to give a clear definition of that notion, addressing how machines and living systems change their internal organization by themselves (Ashby, 1962).

Based on E. Schrödinger's work *What is life?* (1944), H. von Foerster named two main mechanisms in self-organizing systems: the *order from order* and the *order from noise* principles (von Foerster, 2003). In Schrödinger's and von Foerster's essays, systems were considered to be governed by the second law of thermodynamics. H. von Foerster stated that a self-organizing system needs a structured environment, where it can consume energy and order. This means that if a self-organizing system decreases its entropy, at the same time entropy in the environment is increased. Consequently, self-organizing systems are not isolated systems, but systems which interact with their environment. With the "order from noise" principle, H. von Foerster illustrated how noise and disturbances could accelerate the self-organizing process.

Self-organization is still a central issue in system science. For instance, the interdisciplinary research field of *synergetics* (working together) studies general principles of self-organization, which are irrespective to the properties of individual parts of a system (Haken, 2004).

Autopoiesis

Based on the findings of second-order cybernetics, H.R. Maturana and F.J. Varela described living systems from the radical constructivism perspective. They came up with a new term characterizing such systems, *autopoiesis*, which denotes "self-producing" (Maturana et al., 1980). They defined several characteristics with which a system must comply to be an autopoietic system. Among others, these are:

- The system must have identifiable boundaries.
- The system is made of constitutive components.
- Properties and characteristics of the system emerge from the interaction of its components.

- The boundary of the system is formed by the interaction and relationships of its components.
- Components are reproduced internally, either directly or indirectly, through transformation of external "consumed" components. This is also called *operational closure*.

Autopoietic systems are therefore recursively organized. That is, the product of the interaction of their components is exactly the organization that produces the components. H.R. Maturana and F.J. Varela (1988) provided a strict definition of life with the concept of autopoietic systems. Consequently, viruses, and most man-made systems, are clearly defined as non-living systems. Whereas biological cells are considered as first-order autopoietic systems, multicellular organisms are regarded as second-order autopoietic systems.

Among others, F.J. Varela was concerned with the question of how autopoietic systems perceive and internalize their environment. Whereas representational approaches look at knowledge as a capacity of the mind to reflect the real world, constructive approaches define cognition as a capacity to give meaning to the reality. A living being gains its knowledge through an incremental learning process based on perception and action. The concept of *enaction* developed by F.J. Varela et al. (1993) follows this principle and encompasses two points: "(1) perception consists in perceptually guided action and (2) cognitive structures emerge from the recurrent sensorimotor patterns that enable action to be perceptually guided" (p. 173). Enaction is the result of a circular process where action and perception are interdependent and influence each other. Intentional actions lead to a perception that is biased by the expected results. The expected result, the perceived state and the performed action in combination leads to cognition. For cognitive living systems, these aspects are inseparable and evolve together. This evolutionary process can be seen as "learning-by-doing". Enaction, also called "faire-émerger" (do-emerge) by F.J. Varela, goes beyond emergentism, which considers emergence as a sufficient mechanism for explaining the construction of complex systems and of cognition starting from elementary laws (Varela et al., 1993, p. 8).

The concept of autopoiesis has also been adopted for studying complex social systems. Each social system possesses its own identity, which is produced by communication between its components (humans). N. Luhmann (2008) pointed out that operational closure does not mean causal isolation, nor that the system possesses all causes of its self-production. It rather expresses that the system has sufficient own causes to perform self-production under the assumption of constant or repeated environmental conditions.

Conversation Theory

Learning is a broad research field, which is also targeted by cybernetics. In the 1960's, G. Pask conceived and developed a cybernetic and dialectic framework from his work on instructional design and the models of individual learning styles. This framework offered a scientific theory, called *conversation theory* (CT) (Pask, 1975), which explains how interaction between entities can lead to construction of shared knowledge and intersubjectivity. Two cognitive systems, like a student and a teacher, or two distinct perspectives within a person's mind, participate in a conversation sharing a given concept. In this conversational process, each participant identifies differences of understanding and attempts to solve them by exchange of meaning. As a consequence, both participants are able to learn from the other's behavior. Finally, the process may end on an implicit or explicit shared agreement of understanding.

G. Pask's work also had an influence on the social sciences. As B. Scott (1980) mentioned, "Pask is unique in having developed a set of concepts which can unify the social sciences: organisationally, a social institution and an isolated psyche are both subsumed as conversational processes" (p. 7). Individuals participating in a conversational process belong to a symbolic, language-oriented system, a *social system*. G. Pask distinguished between two types of self-replicating individuals: (1) mechanical individuals (*M*-individuals) denote operationally closed processors, such as biological organisms. And (2), psychological individuals (*P*-individuals) denote a coherent cognitive organization, which is embedded in an *M*-individual for execution and replication. According to CT, at least one of the participants of a conversation must be a *P*-individual (Pask, 1975, p. 164f).

G. Pask was not just a theorist. His theory was the result of numerous experiments and prototypes. For instance, together with R. McKinnon-Wood he built the Self-Adaptive Keyboard Instructor (SAKI) in 1956 (G. Pask, McKinnon-Wood & E. Pask, 1961). SAKI was designed to teach people how to increase the speed and the quality of typing. Unlike other teaching systems at that time, which followed a learn-by-rote model, SAKI mimics a dynamic relationship between student and teacher. This means that a teacher responds directly to the needs of the student, especially when it is obvious that the student has difficulty understanding certain concepts. For this, SAKI uses an individualized record to evaluate each word and to store the success of the student. Depending on the student, the word and the history, SAKI changes the pace and displayed hints. The way Pask's machines interacted with human beings is still inspiring for human-centered system design. Or as U. Haque (2007) puts it, "Pask's approach, if implemented, would provide a crucial counterpoint to the current pervasive computing approach that is founded on interaction loops that have been fixed by the designer and, if implemented, would have a positive impact on the design of future environments" (p. 8).

CT was further developed and applied to different domains like computer science and design. P. Pangaro demonstrated it with THOUGHTSTICKER, a software that simulates parts of CT. Originally initiated by G. Pask, THOUGHTSTICKER is an information management system based on the principles of conversation. This early information browser had the look-and-feel of modern web browsers. However, it differed from the world wide web in the way information was structured. Other than the anarchic linking of contents using hyperlinks, THOUGHTSTICKER used *entailment meshes* to link content dynamically and user dependently (Pangaro, 1987). Based on this work, P. Pangaro also presented modeling techniques for conversation that hold beyond software engineering (Pangaro, 1989). They help to ensure that a concrete implementation follows the principles of Pask's conversation theory.

H. Dubberly and P. Pangaro applied CT in the context of design. They pointed out that it is important to use the concept of conversation for system design, by proposing to consider every user as a participant in a conversation process between designers and the users (Dubberly et al., 2009). They contrasted conversation with communication. Systems based on the communication model of C.E. Shannon et al. (1949) are limited, because the information source is only able to select messages from a known and predefined set of possible messages. This leads to the limitation that it is impossible to say something novel to someone else. Conversely, conversation allows to share new ideas, concepts and goals. Here, knowledge can evolve and a mutual agreement of common understanding can be reached. They argued that conversation in general allows coordinating "actions in ways that are mutually beneficial for all participating entities. In practice, society is a complex market of coordination based on conversation and conversation is the primary mechanism for complex social coordination. It is a highly effective form of bio-cost reduction and therefore an engine of society" (Dubberly et al., 2009).

G. Pask's and P. Pangaro's work had a great impact on the generic system model developed in our research work. CT is a cornerstone in URANOS, especially in modeling human-human and human-machine collaboration. We believe that the principle of CT will lead to a new era in human-machine interaction, where people and machines together form a learning organization.

SYSTEMICS

The term "systemics" refers to holistic and generic approaches in the context of studying systems. Systems thinking is more a transversal or meta discipline than a discipline by itself. It involves different research domains such as philosophy, cybernetics, management and organization, biology, mathematics and physics. Great philosophers from ancient days contributed to systems thinking, like Lao, Plato and Aristotle. The term "systemics" was elaborated by M. Bunge in the 1970s. He used it to refer to the various systems theories describing systems generically and thus contributed to overcoming the artificial barriers between disciplines (Bunge, 1979).

In terms of systems thinking, an extensive map of related work and their influences is presented by the International Institute for General Systems Studies (2001)[1]. This map was originated by E. Schwarz in 1996. It includes the influences of researchers in the domains of mathematics, physics, computer science, engineering, cybernetics, systemics, biology, ecology, sociology and philosophy from ancient times to the present. This section presents some of this work, which had significant influence on the research and development of URANOS.

System Theories

When L. von Bertalanffy first introduced the *General System Theory* (GST) in 1968, he intended to provide abstractions and conceptual models which enable interdisciplinary collaboration, helping to approach complex and cross-domain problems. He realized that several research disciplines were facing similar challenges dealing with complex and non-linear systems. But, it was difficult to have a conversation between the different research communities because each one used a different language and terminology to address their problems and solutions. With GST, a general language was developed to overcome this issue. Ever since, GST has become an important means to ensuring that theories can unite in the nonphysical fields of science.

GST is related to cybernetics. As stated by L. von Bertalanffy (1968), *"cybernetics, e.g., proved its impact not only in technology but in basic sciences, yielding models for concrete phenomena and bringing teleological phenomena - previously tabooed - into the range of scientifically legitimate problems"* (p. 23). But GST chose a different approach. L. von Bertalanffy argued that (first-order) cybernetics did not replace the mechanistic view and machine theory. Rather, it extended this view. He aimed to provide a new world view, a general science of "wholeness" addressing universal principles that apply to systems in general.

In the 1980's D. Julong initiated the *Gray System Theory*. The goal was to fill the gap between social and natural sciences. In this sense, gray means that some of the components, relations or dynamics are unknown, incomplete or uncertain (Julong, 1982, 1989). Gray system models help to study problems, even if there is only inadequate and incomplete information available, that is incomplete knowledge about a system's components, structure, boundary and behavior. In reality, all systems can be considered as gray systems, just because an observer can never perceive all system events. Even if a deterministic program is running on a computer, unforeseen states can occur, for example due to hardware errors, time delays or external disturbances. The theory was further developed and specified by S. Liu and Y. Lin. Their comprehensive work on gray systems and their application to game theory, decision-making and control systems was presented in their book *Grey Systems: Theory and Applications* (Liu & Lin, 2011).

Non-linearity in evolutionary processes was studied and described by S. OuYang et al. (2001) in their *blown-up theory*. Blown-ups are transitional changes in a discontinued evolution process, that is a dramatic and irregular change in the system's structure. The goal of the theory is to provide methods to predict forthcoming blown-ups more accurately, as well as what comes after such changes.

Gray system theory and blown-up theory led to a new way of understanding complex and non-linear systems and their evolutionary development. Y. Lin (2008) proposed a new systemic model based on these theories, called the *systemic yoyo model*. Each system is regarded as a multidimensional spinning entity (in the three-dimensional space resembling a Chinese yoyo). At one end it consumes entities (physical, informational etc.), whereas on the other end it spits them out. Some of the entities are in a close loop as they are consumed several times, others are not. Using this model, Y. Lin intend to improve forecasts in complex and non-linear systems, like meteorology and economy.

Systems Thinking

Closely related to GST is the systems philosophy, which deals with the nature of complexity and wholeness. It led to systems thinking, which asked for a different approach to analyze and study complex systems. Rather than the rational cartesian analysis, where systems are broken down into entities and considered in isolation, early approaches of GST tended to invoke the principles of holism. That is, explanation is sought on the level of totality. But, as mentioned by E. Morin, this approach is insufficient to explain the nature of complexity. He claimed that a system should not be reduced to totality. It must be seen in the context of complexity of whole and parts. He suggested an approach of distinguishing and linking. Entities should be distinguished from each other, but their relationship to one another must be taken into account in order to understand them in the context of the whole (Morin, 2006).

Morin's approach is to consider the whole and its parts simultaneously - "to know the parts through the whole; to know the whole through the parts" (Morin, 1992). He described the complex relation between whole and parts, which includes the following three points:

1. The whole is greater than the sum of its parts, because new properties and qualities emerge through the interaction of the parts.
2. The whole is less than the sum of its parts, because certain properties of the parts can be suppressed within the whole.
3. The whole is greater than the whole, because the parts are affected retroactively by the totality (Morin, 1992).

K. Wilber has a similar argument. As an exponent of integral thinking, he developed, in addition to the integral philosophy, models for complex systems. As one of his integral thinking tenets, he stated that the world is made of holons, entities that are wholes and parts simultaneously. They emerge in hierarchies, called holarchies, a term he borrowed from A. Koestler (1976). In contrast to conventional hierarchies, "each deeper or higher holon embraces its junior predecessors and then adds its own new and more encompassing pattern or wholeness - the new code or canon or morphic field or agency that will define this as a whole and not merely a heap (as Aristotle clearly spotted)" (Wilber, 1995, p. 75). With AQAL, he developed an integral model explaining entities from four perspectives: objective, subjective, interobjective and intersubjective standpoint. This model is presented in more details in section "Integral Thinking" in chapt. "Model Instantiations".

Systems and integral thinking influenced the latest approaches in designing and engineering. For instance, A. Ninck et al. (2001) presented methodologies for analyzing complex problems and finding viable solutions. In this sense, an attempt was made to solve engineering tasks holistically under the consideration of sustainability, humanity and economy.

Systemic Metamodel

A model for viable natural systems was proposed by E. Schwarz (2002). In this model, he accommodated the different systemic perspectives and aspects of complex and non-linear systems in a comprehensive and holistic metamodel. His approach is unique in terms of combining various epistemological viewpoints such as reductionism and holism in one model. He defined three planes, each one describing a dimension of the system (Figure 3). The first plane (plane of energy) corresponds to the world of physics. The second plane (plane of information) describes the cybernetical world made of relations and potentialities. On the last plane (plane of totality) a holistic being appears in its existential dimension (Schwarz, 2002; Schwarz, 2010).

The model describes the dynamics of any complex living system through six logical loops. The horizontal loops (vortices, homeostasis and self-reference) are responsible for stability. The vertical loops (morphogenesis, autopoiesis and autogenesis) are responsible for changes, growth and autonomy.

Figure 3. Model of a viable natural system made of three planes; the plane of energy corresponding to physics, the plane of information describing the relations and potentialities, and the plane of totality containing the aspects that emerge through the totality of the system (Schwarz, 2002).

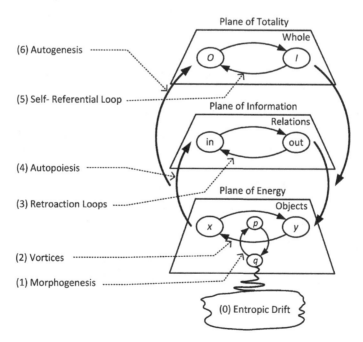

Figure 4. Spiral of self-organization describing the evolutionary development process of a system. Each stage leads to a more complex and autonomous behavior (Schwarz, 2002).

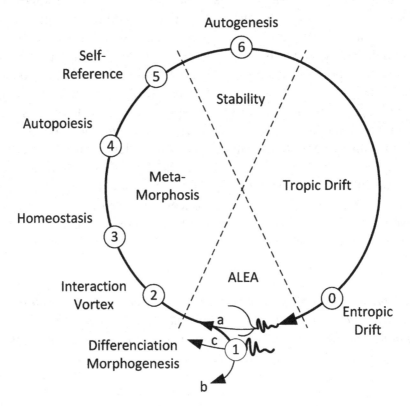

Further, E. Schwarz focused on the phenomena and stages that lead to complexity and self-organization. His spiral of self-organization describes how a system can develop its organization (Figure 4). Each stage leads to more complex and autonomous behavior during the system's long term evolution. These stages correspond to the appearance of the six logical loops.

- **Entropic Drift (0):** A natural trend which can drive the system far from equilibrium. It corresponds to a trend toward the more probable, meaning an increase of entropy and an actualization of potentialities.
- **Morphogenesis (1):** In this stage, a reinforcing feedback loop amplifies small fluctuations. Simple structures emerge on the physical plane differentiating themselves from the medium through some basic interaction between them.

- **Interaction Vortex (2):** While physical entities interact with each other, relations emerge on the information plane. These relations characterize the system dynamics, acquiring a certain stability due to the circularity, e.g. there is a cyclic exchange of energy and matter (vortices).
- **Homeostasis (3):** In this stage the system starts to regulate itself. The regulation is based on dampening feedback loops between the physical and information planes. For example, some physical parameters are regulated, like temperature or pressure. On the totality plane the object (physical structure) and its image (network of potentialities) start to reference each other.
- **Autopoiesis (4):** A system reaching this stage is able to maintain not only parameters but also structures through the interaction between the physical and information planes. The system becomes capable of producing itself, meaning it incarnates a network of causality which can produce the system.
- **Self-Reference (5):** The system starts to reference its own image. The degree of self-reference can be interpreted as the level of consciousness.
- **Autogenesis (6):** This stage leads to the autonomy of a system. It becomes a "being", which refers to the ability to create its own laws.

A system can go through these stages several times (spiral). After reaching the stability stage, noise can lead to actualization of potentialities or disposition of the system. In the "Alea", the system does not necessarily end up with a new viable system (a), but can destroy itself (b), or can continue with minor changes (c).

Our approach has been strongly influenced by the proposal of E. Schwarz. We let ourselves be inspired by the concepts of autopoiesis, autogenesis and self-referencing. In contrast to his approach, we go beyond physical or natural systems and look at systems in general from an objective, a subjective and a holistic perspective. Further, we aim to develop a model which is able to handle new epistemological perspectives in the future by adding additional planes.

Generic Agency Model

E. Schwarz's systemic metamodel inspired M. Yolles and G. Fink when defining their generic agency theory. They proposed a generic modeling approach for living systems theory and showed how higher cybernetic orders promote simpler modeling, even as the complexity of the system increases (Yolles & Fink, 2014). In their model, an operative system (first plane) is

Figure 5. Third order agency model made of three systems, the operative, the figurative and the cognitive system (Yolles & Fink, 2014).

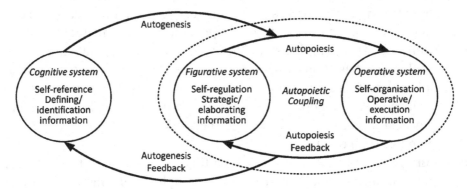

coupled with a figurative system (second plane) by autopoiesis. Similarly, the autopoietic coupling of these two systems is coupled with a cognitive system through autogenesis (Figure 5).

They generalized these couplings between systems (planes) formulating a recursive agency model of *(n+1)*-th order, which is based on *n*-th cybernetic models. The result is an autopoietic hierarchy, where each referent system is coupled with autopoietic coupling of *(n+1)*-th order.

Our model URANOS, described in chapter "URANOS: A Generic System Model", bares resemblance to generic agency theory, since both models generalize the metamodel of E. Schwarz. Our model differs from the agency model as we do not necessarily imply an autopoietic hierarchy, but rather describe the couplings as *emergence/immergence loops*. This is per se not a contradiction to the agency model's autopoietic couplings, but it is more general. Further, our model focuses on symbiotic dynamics between systems. In this sense, it can also be used to examine systems on each plane with respect to collaboration, coordination and social behavior.

COORDINATION

Why is coordination relevant in current system modeling? There are two main reasons to mention coordination in this context. First, coordination is one of many views onto a system. It expresses the management of system evolution and helps to understand the dynamics and organization of complex systems. And second, coordination theories and models were the trigger for our generic system model URANOS. Research on coordination delivered many important concepts to model complex and dynamic systems.

This section gives an evolutionary overview of this research over the last 20 years. It is split into two main parts: coordination theory, and coordination models.

Coordination Theory

Only a few publications address the theoretical and philosophical aspects of coordination. A well-known and often referenced paper in this matter is T.W. Malone and K. Crowston's coordination theory (1994). They built a theoretical framework for coordination that holds beyond computer science. It can be used for many other kinds of research areas like biology, sociology or economics. From their point of view, an organization is understood as a set of actors performing activities and consuming resources. Dependencies arise as soon as activities lead to conflicting interests between actors. K. Crowston (1994) presented a taxonomy of dependencies and the coordination processes managing them. He used a simple ontology, namely the notion of *task* and *resource*. Tasks denote the dynamic part and include goals, motives and activities. Resources on the other hand include everything that is affected by the tasks.

Instead of managing dependencies a system can also handle the opposite, the *power*. The *power-dependence relation* was introduced by R.M. Emerson (1962). He described power not as an attribute of an actor (person), but rather as a property of a social relation between two actors. The dependence of one actor provides the basis for the power of the other actor. But to analyze the power-dependence relation between two actors, the social relationships with other actors must also be taken into account. This is because an actor can join forces with others to expand its power over someone else. The imbalance of power and dependency between actors is one of the motors of evolution, where systems tend to balance their power-dependence relations while they evolve.

Some crucial concepts for coordination, especially subjective and cognitive characteristics of actors, were presented by D.H. Gelernter in *The muse in the machine: Computerizing the Poetry of Human Thought* (1994). Cognitive systems (like humans) are based on a cognitive spectrum ranging from high focus to low focus, like low level attention and dreaming. He stated that creativity may happen in the lower range of the spectrum by the loss of control over the thought stream. Once the actor regains control he becomes aware of the new thoughts that could lead to new and unexpected connections between the starting and ending thoughts. He identified emotions as "a felt state of mind" that helps to glue low-focus thought streams together. Creativity without emotions is not possible. Gelernter's notion of a spectrum as a continuum rather than a discrete range has inspired us to develop our model on spectra.

Coordination Models

One of the first attempts to model coordination was presented by D.H. Gelernter and N. Carriero (1992). They proposed a complete programming model that is made of two separate models: a computation model and a coordination model. The computation model describes computational activities such as information processing. The coordination, on the other hand, is understood as the glue fitting computational activities together, forming a complete program. The coordination model is embodied by a coordination language that manages the communication between activities. That means, the problems, which are solved using a coordination language are *orthogonal* to the ones solved by the computational language. The decoupling of computation and coordination helps to design, to implement and to maintain complex computational systems. Computational activities could be easily and dynamically reconfigured by coordination in to new assemblies leading to new overall behaviors.

Studying coordination has been one of the main tasks in our research group for over two decades. The following contributions show the evolutionary research in our group that significantly influenced this work.

It started in the early 90's, when the coordination language *CoLa* was developed by B. Hirsbrunner et al. (1994). CoLa aims to handle coordinative aspects in massively parallel environments for distributed artificial intelligence applications. The model expresses the use of a wide range of communication protocols based on topologies, and formalizes the notion of a communication medium. Fundamental principles in CoLa are *the point of view* and *the range of vision*, which describe the local view of an agent onto the global communication environment (Renevey, Aguilar, Hirsbrunner & Krone, 1995a). This is due to the impossibility of keeping a global communication state in each agent, especially when dealing with large complex systems. These principles are some of the main differences with other coordination models at that time, but were later used and extended in many coordination models including our system generic model.

With ϕ-CoLa a first attempt was made by C. Renevey & M. Courant (1995b) to integrate the physical dimension (ϕ) into the computing space. The model was oriented towards highly dynamic systems and complex system organization describing the characteristics of logical-physical world interactions. Our vision to handle all entities of a complex system with a generic model is rooted in their approach. C. Renevey et al. argued that "the generic concepts we put forward here can adapt to heterogeneous physical spaces and open up to a unified coordination between agents of a different nature: logical entities, robots and human beings..." (Renevey & Courant, 1995b, p. 2).

Based on CoLa and the insights of the research on coordination a new model was developed by O. Krone et al. (1998), called the *encapsulation coordination model* (ECM). The model was embodied in the coordination language STL[2] and verified in massive number crunching and multi-agent systems (MASs). The model follows the paradigm that a coordination model in computer science must encompass at least four components, namely: entities, media, law and tools. In ECM the coordination entities are *processes* that can be hierarchically structured in the coordination space through *blobs*. Blobs allow to group processes and to encapsulate them from other processes. The dynamic part of ECM is realized through *events*, a mechanism that reacts to new happenings inside a blob. Two or more processes can communicate with each other through *connections* which are established between matching *ports*, openings of entities and blobs to the external world. Blobs, events, ports and connections belong to the media enabling to coordinate processes.

As the research and development on coordination progressed, different categories of models emerged. A common classification was to distinguish between data-driven and process-driven coordination (Papadopoulos & Arbab, 1998). A more comprehensive and systemic approach was presented by M. Schumacher. He described coordination from different points of view onto a system, which had a significant impact in system design. Based on the ECM and the study of coordination for MAS, M. Schumacher (2001) identified two types of dependencies that lead to two corresponding levels of coordination, *objective* and *subjective coordination*. Objective coordination manages the inter-agent dependencies that include the organization of the environment and the interaction between agents. Subjective coordination manages the intra-agent dependencies towards other agents. Objective and subjective coordination are related, but at the same time express a complementary view onto the system (Figure 6).

The two levels of coordination were further analyzed by other research groups, like A. Omicini et al. They stated that objective coordination relies on the point of view of an external observer who inspects and designs coordination artifacts (processes, rules) in order to achieve his goals. On the other hand, subjective coordination is expressed by agents from their point of view, which is biased and subjective due to its individual perception and

Figure 6. Objective and subjective coordination (Schumacher, 2001; Omicini et al., 2003b).

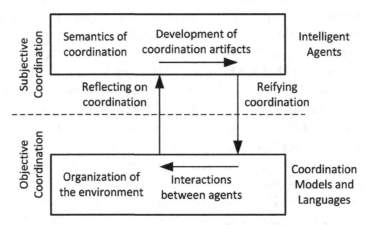

knowledge about the system (Omicini & Ossowski, 2003a; Omicini, Ricci, Rimassa & Viroli, 2003b).

A generic semantic coordination model was formulated by A. Tafat et al. (2005), called XCM. It was a first attempt to establish a universal coordination model for pervasive computing. The model is expressed as an ontology that allows a shared understanding between interactive partners about environmental and contextual knowledge. The three characteristics of XCM are: (1) homogeneous management of contextual dynamics, (2) genericity through the notion of "everything is an entity", and (3) handling dynamics in physical and virtual environments likewise. The ontology of XCM denotes entities as a first-level notion. The notion of an environment prescribes the dynamics and the structure of contained entities through physical and social laws. Finally, the notion of ports enables the communication between two interacting entities.

With pervasive and mobile computing new approaches were needed, like coordination within service oriented and smart environments. S. Maffioletti (2006) introduced a unified model for pervasive and heterogeneous systems, called UbiDEV. Following the principles of autopoiesis (Maturana et al.,1980) the model describes the pervasive computing system as a cognitive system based on perceiving (observing), representing and acting (Figure 7). Its internal structure is adapted to observed changes in the environment which is enriched with adequate services and interaction models afterwards.

Figure 7. A generic model of a cognitive system (Maffioletti, 2006).

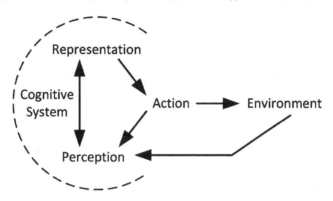

Based on the General System Theory (Bertalanffy, 1968) P. Bruegger formulated a holistic model for proactive observation. It contains three elements:

1.   A set of entities (environment and observables),
2.   Observers and
3.   Viewers.

In this sense, a system is understood as an observed environment. An observer perceives the observed entities through its viewers, which define the scope of the observation. The observer has two possibilities. Either he reports the observed situation to a dedicated application, or he directly generates a feedback made of actions that are then performed within an environment. In his work, new concepts were introduced, like "a situation is made of context and activity", and the way raw data is sensed and abstracted (Bruegger, 2011). That crucially influenced our work, especially how observation is understood and modeled.

SUMMARY

This chapter presented some of the relevant aspects and related work of generic system modeling. Three domains are presented which influenced our work the most: cybernetics, systemics and coordination.

Cybernetics is the study of system governance and system dynamics. It describes controlling, learning and collaboration from a generic standpoint. Many of the cybernetic tenets were adopted by other scientific domains.

Therefore, lots of generic system theories and models are based today on the results and achievements of cybernetics. In the beginning, the focus was on feedback and control loops. This so called first-order cybernetics was soon extended by a new model including the observer as an integral component. This approach was referred to as second-order cybernetics. In this context, self-organizing systems, autopoiesis and conversation theory (CT) were presented, each one being an important cornerstone of URANOS.

Systemics brought a new way of seeing systems to the research communities. In contrast to reductionistic and mechanistic approaches, systemics treat system as a whole. That is, aspects are taken into account, which only appear in the totality of the system. But, one has to be careful that holism does not lead to reductionistic system analyses, as criticized by E. Morin (1992). As shown by E. Schwarz, living systems require multiple epistemological standpoints included in one model. He proposed to handle physical, logical and holistic aspects on different planes. Our approach adopted and generalized this model. We aimed to handle multiple standpoints, such as objectivism, subjectivism and holism, within one model.

Inspiration and concepts of our generic system model URANOS are also rooted in the research on coordination. Theories and models of coordination were presented that inspired and engaged this work. Additionally, an evolutionary overview on the research of this topic over the last twenty years was given. URANOS differs from these coordination models, as it is more generic and addresses system dynamics beyond coordination aspects.

Many of the insights gained by cybernetics, systemics and coordination research lead to the model we propose for human-centered systems.

REFERENCES

Ashby, W. R. (1957). *An introduction to Cybernetics*. London, UK: Chapman and Hall.

Ashby, W. R. (1962). Principles of the Self-organizing System. In H. von Foerster & G. W. Zopf (Eds.), *Principles of Self-Organization:Transactions of the University of Illinois Symposium* (pp. 255-278). London, UK: Pergamon.

Bruegger, P. (2011). *uMove: a wholistic framework to design and implement ubiquitous computing systems supporting user's activity and situation* (Doctoral dissertation). Retrieved from réro Doc. (R006095784)

Bunge, M. (1979). *Treatise on Basic Philosophy: Ontology II: A World of Systems*. Springer. doi:10.1007/978-94-009-9392-1

Crowston, K. (2003). A Taxonomy of Organizational Dependencies and Coordination Mechanisms. In T. W. Malone, W. Thomas, K. Crowston, & G. Herman (Eds.), *Organizing Business Knowledge: The MIT Process Handbook*. Cambridge, MA: The MIT Press.

Dubberly, H., & Pangaro, P. (2009). On Modeling - What is conversation, and how can we design for it? *Interaction*, *16*(4), 22–28. doi:10.1145/1551986.1551991

Emerson, R. M. (1962). Power-Dependence Relations. *American Sociological Review*, *27*(1), 31–41. doi:10.2307/2089716

Gelernter, D. H. (1994). *The Muse in the Machine: Computerizing the Poetry of Human Thought*. New York, NY: The Free Press.

Gelernter, D. H., & Carriero, N. (1992). Coordination Languages and their Significance. *Communications of the ACM*, *35*(2), 97–107. doi:10.1145/129630.129635

Haken, H. (2004). *Synergetics - Introduction and Advanced Topics*. Berlin, Germany: Springer.

Haque, U. (2007). The Architectural Relevance of Gordon Pask. *Architectural Design*, *77*(4), 45–61. doi:10.1002/ad.487

Hirsbrunner, B., Aguilar, M., & Krone, O. (1994). CoLa: A Coordination Language for Massive Parallelism. In *Proceedings ACM Symposium on Principles of Distributed Computing (PODC)*. New York, NY: ACM. doi:10.1145/197917.198156

International Institute for General Systems Studies. (2001). *Some Streams of Systemic Thought*. Neuchâtel, Switzerland: Author.

Julong, D. (1982). Control problems of grey systems. *Systems & Control Letters*, *1*(5), 288–294. doi:10.1016/S0167-6911(82)80025-X

Julong, D. (1989). Introduction to Grey System Theory. *Journal of Grey System*, *1*(1), 1–24.

Koestler, A. (1967). *The Ghost in the Machine*. London, UK: Hutchinson.

Krippendorff, K. (1986). *A Dictionary of Cybernetics*. Norfolk, VA: American Society for Cybernetics.

Krone, O., Chantemargue, F., Dagaeff, T., & Schumacher, M. (1998). Coordinating Autonomous Entities with STL. *SIGAPP Appl. Comput. Rev.*, 6(2), 18–32. doi:10.1145/297114.297118

Lin, Y. (2008). *Systemic Yoyos: Some Impacts of the Second Dimension.* London, UK: CRC Press. doi:10.1201/9781420088212

Liu, S., & Lin, Y. (2011). *Grey Systems: Theory and Applications.* Berlin, Germany: Springer. doi:10.1007/978-3-642-16158-2

Luhmann, N. (2008). *Soziologische Aufklärung 6 - Die Soziologie und der Mensch* (3rd ed.). VS Verlag für Sozialwissenschaften.

Maffioletti, S. (2006). *UbiDev: A Homogeneous Service Framework for Pervasive Computing Environments* (Doctoral dissertation). Retrieved from réro Doc. (R004526374)

Malone, T. W., & Crowston, K. (1994). The Interdisciplinary Study of Coordination. *ACM Computing Surveys*, 26(1), 87–119. doi:10.1145/174666.174668

Maturana, H. R., & Varela, F. J. (1988). *The Tree of Knowledge: The Biological Roots of Human Understanding* (1st ed.). Boston, MA: New Science Library.

Maturana, H. R., Varela, F. J., & Beer, S. (1980). *Autopoiesis and Cognition: The Realization of the Living* (1st ed.). Springer. doi:10.1007/978-94-009-8947-4

Morin, E. (1992). From the Concept of System to the Paradigm of Complexity. *Journal of Social and Evolutionary Systems*, 15(4), 371–385. doi:10.1016/1061-7361(92)90024-8

Morin, E. (2006). Restricted Complexity, General Complexity. In C. Gershenson, D. Aerts, & B. Edmonds (Eds.), *Worldviews, Science and Us: Philosophy and Complexity* (pp. 5–29). World Scientific.

Ninck, A., Bürki, L., Hungerbühler, R., & Mühlemann, H. (2001). *Systemik - Integrales Denken, Konzipieren und Realisieren* (3rd ed.). Zurich, Switzerland: Verlag Industrielle Organisation.

Omicini, A., & Ossowski, S. (2003a). Objective versus Subjective Coordination in the Engineering of Agent Systems. In M. Klusch, S. Bergamaschi, P. Edwards, & P. Petta (Eds.), *Intelligent Information Agents* (Vol. 2586, pp. 179–202). Berlin, Germany: Springer. doi:10.1007/3-540-36561-3_9

Omicini, A., Ricci, A., Rimassa, G., & Viroli, M. (2003b). *Integrating Objective & Subjective Coordination in FIPA: A Roadmap to TuCSoN. AI*IA/ TABOO Joint Workshop "From Objects to Agents", WOA'03*. Villasimius, CA, Italy: Pitagora Editrice Bologna.

OuYang, S., Lin, Y., Wang, Z., & Peng, T. (2001). Blown-up theory of evolution science and fundamental problems of the first push. *Kybernetes, 30*(4), 448–462. doi:10.1108/03684920110386955

Pangaro, P. (1987). *An Examination and Confirmation of a Macro Theory of Conversations through A Realization of the Protologic Lp by Microscopic Simulation*. Retrieved from Brunel University Research Archive: http://bura. brunel.ac.uk/handle/2438/5320

Pangaro, P. (1989). *The Architecture of Conversation Theory*. Retrieved from http://www.pangaro.com/L1L0/ArchCTBriefly2b.htm

Papadopoulos, G. A., & Arbab, F. (1998). *Coordination Models and Languages. Advances in Computers*. Academic Press.

Pask, G. (1975). *Conversation, Cognition and Learning: A Cybernetic Theory and Methodology*. New York, NY: Elsevier Publishing Company.

Pask, G., McKinnon-Wood, R., & Pask, E. (1961). *Patent Specification (866279) for "Apparatus for assisting an operator in performing a skill"*. Retrieved from European Patent Office. (Patent GB866279 (A))

Pias, C. (2016). *Cybernetics: The Macy Conferences 1946-1953. the Complete Transactions*. Zurich, Switzerland: Diaphanes Verlag.

Powers, W. T., Abbott, B., Carey, T. A., Goldstein, D. M., Mansell, W., Marken, R. S., & Taylor, M. et al. (2008). Perceptual Control Theory - A Model for Understanding the Mechanisms and Phenomena of Control. In D. Forssell (Ed.), *Perceptual Control Theory: Science & Applications: A Book of Readings* (pp. 18–34). Living Control Systems Publishing.

Renevey, C., Aguilar, M., Hirsbrunner, B., & Krone, O. (1995a). *COLA: Yet Another Coordination Language. Workshop Parallel-Algorithmen*. Postdam, Germany: Rechnerstrukturen und-Systemsoftware.

Renevey, C., & Courant, M. (1995b). Phi-CoLa: Towards a Logico-Physical Coordination Language. *Proceedings of the Workshop on Future and Practice of Autonomous Systems*. Monte Verita, Switzerland: FPAS'95.

Schrödinger, E. (1944). *What is Life? The Physical Aspect of the Living Cell*. Cambridge, UK: Cambridge University Press.

Schumacher, M. (2001). *Objective Coordination in Multi-Agent System Engineering: Design and Implementation*. Berlin, Germany: Springer-Verlag. doi:10.1007/3-540-44933-7

Schwarz, E. (2002). Can Real Life Complex Systems Be Interpreted with the Usual Dualist Physicalist Epistemology - Or is a Holistic Approach Necessary? *Proceedings of the fifth European Systems Science Congress*, *2*, 1-9.

Schwarz, E., & Dubois, D. M. (2010). On the Nature of Consciousness - On Consciousness in Nature. *AIP Conference Proceedings*, *1303*, 334–342. doi:10.1063/1.3527171

Scott, B. (1980). The Cybernetics of Gordon Pask - Part 1. *International Cybernetics Newsletter - The ICNL Founding Fathers Series II, 17*, 327-336.

Shannon, C. E., & Weaver, W. (1949). *The Mathematical Theory of Communication*. Urbana, IL: University of Illinois Press.

Sontag, E. D. (1998). *Mathematical Control Theory: Deterministic Finite Dimensional Systems* (2nd ed.). New York, NY: Springer-Verlag New York, Inc. doi:10.1007/978-1-4612-0577-7

Tafat, A., Courant, M., & Hirsbrunner, B. (2005). Implicit environment-based coordination in pervasive computing. *Proceedings of the 2005 ACM symposium on Applied computing*. New York, NY: ACM. doi:10.1145/1066677.1066781

Varela, F. J., Thompson, E., & Rosch, E. (1993). *The Embodied Mind: Cognitive Science and Human Experience*. Cambridge, MA: The MIT Press.

von Bertalanffy, L. (1968). *General System Theory: Foundations, Development, Applications*. New York, NY: George Braziller Inc.

von Foerster, H. (1992). Ethics and Second Order Cybernetics. *Cybernetics & Human Knowing*, *1*(1), 9–19.

von Foerster, H. (2003). *On Self-Organizing Systems and Their Environments. In Understanding Understanding: Essays on Cybernetics and Cognition* (pp. 1–19). New York, NY: Springer. doi:10.1007/0-387-21722-3_1

Wiener, N. (1948). *Cybernetics: or Control and Communication in the Animal and the Machine* (2nd ed.). Cambridge, MA: MIT Press.

Wiener, N. (1950). *The Human Use of Human Beings: Cybernetics and Society*. Boston, MA: Houghton Mifflin.

Wilber, K. (1995). *Sex, Ecology, Spirituality: The Spirit of Evolution*. Boston, MA: Shambhala Publications.

Yolles, M., & Fink, G. (2014). *Generic Agency Theory, Cybernetic Orders and New Paradigms*. Retrieved from http://papers.ssrn.com/sol3/papers.cfm?abstract_id=2463270

ENDNOTES

[1] Updated version including the contribution of our research: appendix "Some Streams of Systemic Thought".

[2] Simple Thread Language (STL), which was based on C, managing processes and threads over LAN between different UNIX workstations.

Chapter 2
URANOS:
A Generic System Model

ABSTRACT

This chapter presents a generic system model called URANOS, that allows to design complex human-centered systems. It is not aligned to any particular discipline. Rather, it helps to build integral systems in different domains of science and engineering, even though it was originally intended to participate in the design of complex human-centered systems in the framework of ICT. URANOS aims at encouraging interdisciplinary work and reinforces the understanding of complex systems in general. It combines different epistemological standpoints and their corresponding realities into a wholeness. Concretely, the three fundamental standpoints of objectivism, subjectivism and holism are used to holistically handle all relevant entities such as humans, animals, machines and environments. This chapter also addresses systemic features like consciousness, collaboration and symbiosis providing a generic and abstract understanding of them.

INTRODUCTION

In many sciences, like computer science, biology or sociology, complex and non-linear systems cannot be completely understood in a dualistic world view. This means that certain system properties cannot, or only with difficulty, be described by their models. We propose to use a more comprehensive and generic approach to modeling such systems.

This chapter presents the generic system model, URANOS, that we propose for designing complex human-centered systems. The goal of this

DOI: 10.4018/978-1-5225-1888-4.ch002

model is to look at things holistically. It combines various epistemological standpoints and their corresponding realities into a wholeness. Concretely, the three fundamental standpoints of objectivism, subjectivism and holism are represented. Each of them brings new aspects and dynamics to our system model. URANOS is not aligned to any particular discipline, rather, it helps to build integral systems in different domains of science and engineering, even though it was is originally intended to participate in the design of complex human-centered systems in the framework of ICT. It aims at encouraging interdisciplinary work and reinforces the understanding of complex systems in general. Therefore, systemic features like consciousness, collaboration and symbiosis are described from a generic standpoint.

The chapter starts with the epistemological background in section "About Epistemology". It shows how different epistemological standpoints are combined in URANOS. Sections "First-order: Observable Entities", "Second-order: Smart Entities" and "Third-order: Enactive Entities" present the three systemic orders that result from the three fundamental epistemological standpoints. In section "Entity Collaboration" we show how the dynamics between entities leads to collaboration and symbiosis. The development of complex systems is presented in section "System Development". URANOS is not limited to the three systemic orders. Section "Towards n-th order Systems" illustrates how URANOS can be extended with further epistemological standpoints. Finally, this chapter closes with the summary in section "Summary".

ABOUT EPISTEMOLOGY

Complex systems like living systems, and particularly human beings, can be described from a variety of standpoints. To be able to understand a system as a whole, all these realities have to be taken into account. For example, a person can be described as a physical body, or as a psychic apparatus (Freud, 1993). None of the views are wrong, but none describes the human being completely. To understand human beings all of them must be considered, the body, the mind, and the spirit (Wilber, 2007). The generic approach of URANOS takes on this epistemological insight, in which multiple standpoints and realities can exist in parallel and form a new cosmology.

This approach also leads to the insight that any kind of classification is subjective and incomplete. Subjective, because a classification depends on the standpoint of the observer (e.g. designer, architect, analyst). Incomplete, because no one knows all possible classes, and between two classes an infinite number of other classes could exist, like between two irrational numbers. To manifest these insights, URANOS uses the principle of a spectrum (Gelernter, 1994). While describing our model, just a few aspects on a particular spectrum are presented in more detail, like extrema or endpoints. We implicitly assume that there will be more aspects on that spectrum, but at this stage it does not seem worth mentioning them.

Epistemological Standpoints

We aim to give an overview of the major epistemological standpoints that are used in URANOS. The term "epistemological standpoint" describes a world view, through which someone can attain and explain his knowledge. We use the relevant findings of various epistemological standpoints to create and explain our generic system model. As a foundation of URANOS three principal standpoints were used, namely objectivism, subjectivism and holism.

Objectivism

Objectivism refers to the neutral description of entities, a reality that exists regardless of any observation, interpretation and consciousness (Rand, 1990). Observers are in direct contact with that reality and gain objective knowledge from perception through inductive logic and creating models (Reviews, 2013).

In one extreme objectivism can be understood as a philosophical ideal, which defines a reality completely free of interpretations and consciousness. We prefer to use a more moderate kind of objectivism, which is called *intersubjective objectivity* (Ricketts & Levine, 1996). It designates that several subjects (e.g. researchers) have a common understanding of something.

Subjectivism and Relativism

In fundamental objectivism all observers experience the same reality. We know from our own experience that this, however, is not the case. Each observer has an individual awareness, which determines its reality. Subjectivism describes reality as something which is perceived by an individual and manifests itself in his consciousness (metaphysical subjectivism). In this mindset there is no absolute truth. Each observer has its own point of view that gives a relative and subjective "truth" to himself (relativism) (Renevey, Aguilar, Hirsbrunner & Krone, 1995a).

This leads to the standpoint that knowledge is not extracted from the world, but is constructed through interaction and perception (constructivism) (Varela, Thompson & Rosch, 1993). The focus is not on an ontological and objective reality, but rather a constructed and subjective reality.

Holism

In contrast to reductionist thinking, holism states that complex non-linear systems cannot be fully understood through the study of their components. Some system properties (i.e. behaviors) cannot be deduced from the properties of their components alone (von Bertalanffy, 1968). This means that novel properties can emerge due to complexity. They are called *emergent properties* and are characterized as *supervenient*, because they are distinct from all other properties of the system (Crane, 2001). This refers to the epistemic or ontological irreducibility of emerged properties (emergentism). Therefore, structures and functioning must be considered as a whole - as Aristotle said *"the whole is greater than the sum of its parts"*.

Holism reinforces systems and integral thinking, where a system is regarded as a complex and dynamic whole. This is a process of understanding how parts of a system are related and influence each other, without losing focus of the whole.

Generic Standpoint

The aim of our generic approach is to describe a system as many complementary perspectives, so that we get a more complete system model. We use a framework to describe the different standpoints, their aspects and dynamics. The framework, however, has to be considered independently of the standpoints it includes. We therefore use the term *generic standpoint* to highlight this issue, which can be seen as a kind of meta-epistemological standpoint.

Abstraction Continuum

URANOS is based on the assumption that any system can be defined on an *abstraction continuum* characterizing the levels of abstraction of its parts. A continuum is a spectrum, which might have a beginning point, but then extends to infinity. The beginning of the abstraction continuum denotes the most concrete parts of a system. The farther away from the starting point, the more abstract the constructs of a system are.

Example: A computer system can be defined as a logical process running on a hardware composition. The hardware components are the most concrete objects on the abstraction continuum. Software components like procedures, classes and interface definitions are logical objects of higher abstraction.

Planes

Epistemological standpoints can be mapped to the abstraction continuum. This leads to planes, each describing a reality proposed by the corresponding standpoint. Three planes describe the constructs of objectivism, subjectivism and holism (Figure 1).

The first plane is called the *objective plane*, and describes the reality of the most concrete constructs and is free of interpretations. Subjectivism allows different interpretations of an objective reality, which is mapped to a subjective reality, i.e. an abstract model. The *subjective plane* describes these emerging models. A third plane is needed to describe systems from a holistic standpoint. It is called the *holistic plane*.

Figure 1. Generic standpoint describing the epistemological standpoints and the corresponding abstraction planes

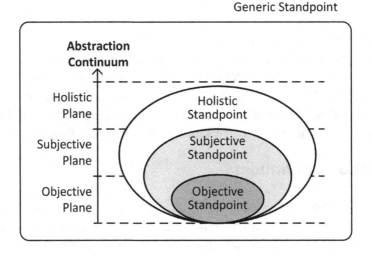

Systemic Orders

Each epistemological standpoint describes a system of a certain order, which encompasses the new epistemological aspects and also encloses the lower ordered system. For instance, a second-order system is described from a subjective standpoint. It encapsulates first-order systems defined by objectivism and extends them through the new findings of subjectivism and relativism. This ordering of systems is called *systemic order*. Accordingly, a system of order n is referred to as an n-th-order system.

Abstraction planes and systemic orders are closely related, but denote different things. The extensions, which are accompanied by n-th-order, are described on the n-th abstraction plane that is associated with the corresponding epistemological standpoint. However, the n-th-order system also encapsulates $(n\text{-}1)$-th-order systems, meaning the lower planes (Figure 2).

Extensibility

URANOS is not limited to three planes and three systemic orders. It can be expanded with additional epistemological standpoints and systemic orders. More comprehensive standpoints describe new aspects on higher abstraction planes, which are encapsulated by the corresponding systemic orders. Thereby, systems of fourth and fifth-order are possible.

Figure 2. Abstraction planes and systemic orders

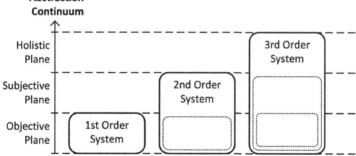

FIRST-ORDER: OBSERVABLE ENTITIES

First-order systems describe the reality from an objective standpoint. This correlates with first-order cybernetics, which characterize well bounded systems that can be observed from the outside.

Example: Often, natural science domains use first-order approaches to model their systems, for instance in physics where models presuppose that there is an objective reality. These models attempt to reproduce reality as accurately as possible.

First-order systems are set on the level of the objective plane. They encompass two fundamental constructs: entities and interactions between entities.

Entity

All nameable things of a system are called *entities*. This includes concrete physical objects and dynamics (e.g. atoms, buildings, natural forces) as well as virtual or abstract constructs (e.g. ideas, thoughts, mathematical formulas).

Definition [Entity]: An entity is anything that actually or potentially exists.

The set of all entities is called the *universe* Ψ. It includes all *actual entities A* and all *potential entities P*:

$$\Psi = A \cup B.$$

Interaction

The principle of interactions is used in many sciences, such as in physics, computer science, biology and sociology. Typically, the term "interaction" refers to correlated actions of two or more entities and it states that these actions have an effect on all participating entities.

URANOS uses this term in a very broad sense. All dynamical phenomena are described through interactions, even those that are not obviously recognizable as such, like observations.

Definition [Interaction]: Interaction is an exchange of anything between
  two or more existing entities.

Assuming there is a set of existing entities E, that is $E \subseteq A$. An interaction i can change this set by changing, adding or removing entities in it. The
set E is changed, resulting in a new set E' (Figure 3). This change is called
transformation. An interaction can thus be understood as a transformation
function in the domain of entities:

$$i : E \subseteq A \subseteq \Psi \rightarrow E' \subseteq A' \subseteq \Psi$$
$$E' = i(E)$$

The transformation i an add entities from the set of potential entities P
to the emerging set of existing entities E'. This refers to the "creation" or
"instantiation" of new entities in E'. In turn i can move entities from E to P'.
This move corresponds to the destruction of existing entities.

Evolution and Time

From the objective standpoint, the continuous change of existing entities
through interactions provokes a system development, which can be described
by the sequencing of interactions, e.g. $E_0 \rightarrow E_1 \rightarrow E_2$ ... This sequence is
called *evolution* ε of E_0. In this context, E_j is called a *state* of the evolution
ε.

Definition [Evolution]: An evolution $\varepsilon(E_X)$ is the sequence of states formed
  by interactions starting at E_x.

Figure 3. Transformation of existing entities E to a new set of existing entities E'
within a universe Ψ

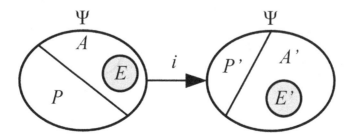

Example: The evolutionary development of living species is one of the most famous evolution models (Darwin, 1859; Dobzhansky, 1937). Here, evolution is a process by which life developed on earth through now extinct species. Decisive in this process is the change in the gene pool through crossing, mutation and selection. The crossing between two individuals and the influence of mutations can be seen as interactions leading to new genomes for a new individual (Mendelian inheritance (Mendel, 1866)). The set of existing genomes E is transformed to new genomes E', which represents a new state of the evolutionary process of species. Selection is an interaction between individuals and their environment. It prefers those that have best adapted to the current state of their population.

Time is a manifestation of the interaction between entities and an epiphenomenon of the evolution. Without interactions, no time would exist. From an objective standpoint, time is denoted as a monotonous non-decreasing function through the ordered sequence of states, e.g. $E_0 \rightarrow E_1 \rightarrow E_2 \ldots$

The evolutionary process can be expressed by the evolution graph of interactions, for example by directed graphs. Vertices denote the states of the evolution and the edges represent the interactions, leading to the corresponding states. Drawing graphs are used to illustrate the evolution (Figure 4).

Subsystems

Interacting entities can be grouped together. These groups form an objective structuring in the universe. There are groups, in between there is no interaction. These groups can be temporarily regarded as closed *subsystems*. In this sense, we use the term "closed" to indicate that there exists no interaction with entities outside that group. And "temporary", because it is not excluded that at some point there will be an interaction between them.

Figure 4. Sequence of states formed by interactions

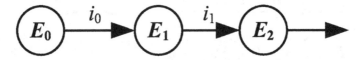

Subsystems can evolve independently of each other. Hence, the evolution is split into several *partial evolution branches*. Each branch has its own sequence of transformations and states. Such branches can merge together once their states become dependent again.

Example: In the evolution of living species, certain species developed independently of each other by spatial separation, for instance in different habitats. This led to great biodiversity. But, it may happen that these separated habitats suddenly come into contact, often through changes in the biosphere or by third parties colonizing both habitats. The result is that their previously independent development paths suddenly become mutually affected. Both evolution branches start to merge together.

Equilibrium

The evolution of the universe (or subsets of the universe) could bring circularity, meaning that a stable state is reached and the evolution process ends (Figure 5a). If the evolution stops at one state or at a set of repeated states, this is called an *equilibrium*. The set of states expressing an equilibrium is called an *attractor* of the dynamics and is denoted as E_A (Heylighen & Joslyn, 2001):

$$\forall E_j \in E_A \land \forall i_x \left\{ i_x : E_j \rightarrow E_A \right\}.$$

The notation of equilibrium is an important characteristic and helps to understand and model stable systems, like control systems and self-organizing systems. The way a system is continuously evolving can be studied in the time-state diagram (Figure 5b). The graph denotes the traversed states (*y*-axes) in relation to time (*x*-axes).

Figure 5. (a) Evolution ends at state E_A; (b) time-state diagram, showing how a system approaches the equilibrium

a)   b)

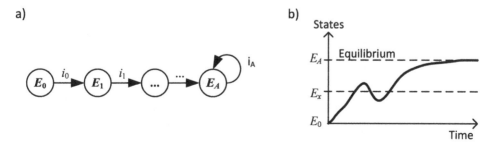

Example: In biology, some creatures have not evolved for millions of years, like the tadpole shrimp, which is one of the oldest living species on earth. Here, the evolution of its genomes stopped 200 million years ago (Kelber, 1999). One can say that their gene pool developed millions of years ago. Since then it remains in a stable state.

Rules

Rules affect evolution by favoring or limiting certain interactions. Without rules, anything could happen in the universe. Through rules the possibilities of evolution are limited, that is to say, certain paths of evolution are prevented (Figure 6).

Definition [Rule]: A rule is a regulation of interaction.

Rules lie on a spectrum from *strong* to *weak*. Strong rules are invariants in the evolutionary process. For instance, the speed of light is a strong rule, an invariant of the physical universe. Another are mathematical axioms, which denote truths in mathematics. Weak rules on the other hand can be created, changed and destroyed during evolution. For instance, social and ethical norms are weak rules that underlie the evolutionary process of human culture.

Interactive System

The model of causality describes what cause led to a particular evolutionary state. The state E_j together with an interaction i are the cause of a new state E_{j+1}, the *effect* of which was provoked by the cause $i(E_j)$.

Figure 6. Rules restrict interaction

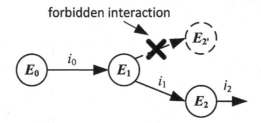

The notion of an *interactive system* (Wirkungsgefüge by Vester (1976)) describes how interacting entities affect each other. It is an abstract description of how evolutionary states are mutually dependent.

There exist two kinds of effects, the reinforcing (positive) and the dampening (negative) effect. The reinforcing effect accelerates evolutionary change in a certain direction. In contrast, the damenping effect slows down the evolution. Cascading two or more effects forms a *causal chain* that has a reinforcing or dampening effect in total.

Feedback Loops

Feedback loops are closed causal chains (circularity). They are of special interest when modeling complex systems, since many of the fundamental phenomena, like self-organization, system governance and learning, are based on circularity. From the objective standpoint two kinds of feedback loops are distinguished: reinforcing and dampening feedback (Forrester, 1969)[1]. In reality, these two kinds often interfere with each other.

A dampening feedback loop has a balancing effect, stabilizing the system. The result is an evolutionary process that approaches towards a stable equilibrium (Figure 7a).

Example: In nature the number predators is stabilized by a dampening feedback loop. If the number of prey animals decreases, some predators will starve, and finally their number also decreases. Thus, more prey animals will survive, which in turn will provoke an increase in predators. The relation between prey animals and predators is in a stable equilibrium.

A reinforcing feedback on the other hand drives the system far from equilibrium through its reinforcing effect (Figure 7b). It is responsible for explosive growth and differentiation. If the system is exposed to reinforcing feedback loops, then its equilibrium is necessarily unstable. A small triggering fluctuation can cause a runaway from that equilibrium, which will never stop. However, reinforcing feedbacks are often accompanied by dampening feedbacks.

Example: The chain reaction in nuclear fission is a reinforcing feedback loop. Enough neurons are released in one fission that cause further fissions. But this process is also accompanied by a dampening feedback causing the fission process to stop, when all nuclear material has been consumed.

Figure 7. (a) Dampening feedback responsible for system stabilization. (b) Reinforcing feedback causing a runaway from equilibrium

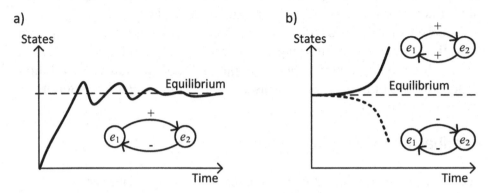

Interaction-Loops

Superposition of several feedback loops ends in very complex circuits. They are responsible for maintaining and evolving the entire system. In total, these circuits are consolidated as an *interaction-loop* that describes all dynamics from the objective standpoint.

Example: The interaction between two states can, for example, consist of economic cooperation and escalating political conflicts. Economic cooperation can be described as a dampening feedback, where trade is dominated by supply and demand. Escalating conflicts on the other hand are reinforcing feedback loops. This leads to an interaction loop which includes both aspects and describes the relationship between states.

Entities and interaction-loops form a well bounded system, called an *observable entity e_o*. It describes an objective reality that can be perceived and interpreted by observers. The most trivial observable entity is made of two interacting entities e_1 and e_2 (Figure 8). We use this simplification for further explanations and sketches of URANOS knowing that Real World Models require much more complex structures.

SECOND-ORDER: SMART ENTITIES

Systems containing intelligent individuals cannot be described and modeled solely by objectivism. Each individual has his own view of the objective

Figure 8. An observable entity e_O made of two interacting entities e_1 and e_2

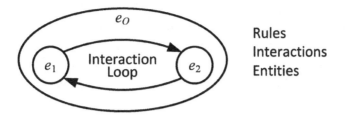

e_1, e_2 : Interacting entities
e_O : Observable entity

reality and acts differently accordingly. This means that reality is partially perceived, and no individual knows the absolute truth.

Example: Physics is a subjective perspective onto the objective reality, which is maintained by a collective of physicians. As A. Einstein said, *"the real difficulty lies in the fact that physics is a kind of metaphysics; physics describes 'reality'. But we do not know what 'reality' is; we know it only by means of the physical description!" (Letter Einstein to Schroedinger, June 1935).*

Modeling systems with intelligent entities requires a paradigm shift, in which the subjectivity of individuals has to be considered. This leads to second-order system models. The observer is no longer an external entity outside of the system, but enters into his own observation (von Foerster, 1992). A second-order system takes into account two planes, the objective and the subjective. The objective plane still represents the objective reality. The subjective plane in turn describes the individual view on that reality. Second-order systems are called *smart entities*.

Topology

The most fundamental process of subjectivity is the attribution of entities. It allows to compare entities qualitatively and to create any relationships among them. Entities can now be arranged under different aspects, such as space-, time- and logical-relations. Such an arrangement is called a *topology of entities*.

Attributes and Relations

For humans, it is natural to bring entities together in relationships. For instance, "the color of this ball is blue" is characterizing a physical entity "ball" through another entity "blue". In this context "blue" is an entity that describes the ball. We call the describing entity an *attribute*.

Definition[Attribute]: If an entity describes another entity, it is called an attribute.

If two or more entities share attributes, then they are in relation to each other with respect to these attributes. Many entities could share the attribute "blue", with the result that all these entities are brought into relation. A set of "blue entities" is created.

Definition [Relation]: If two or more entities share some attributes, the sharing is called a relation.

A relationship may comprise an arbitrary number of entities. A relation L between two entities e_1 and e_2 is called a *binary relation* and is denoted by $L(e_1, e_2)$. Let $A(e_i)$ be the set of all attributes of the entity e_i then:

$$A(e_1) \cap A(e_2) \neq \varnothing \leftrightarrow L(e_1, e_2).$$

Generalized, an *n-ary relation L* is denoted by $L(e_1, e_2, \ldots e_n)$. Accordingly, L only exists if there is at least one shared attribute among $e_1, e_2, \ldots e_n$:

$$\bigcap_{i=1}^{n} A(e_i) \neq \varnothing \leftrightarrow L(e_1, e_2, \ldots e_n).$$

Attributes and relations are the structural primitives on the subjective plane. Other more complex subjective constructs are made of these primitives.

Situation

From a subjective standpoint, the current state of an entity is called *situation S*. There is a significant difference between the "state" and "situation". The state describes a set of existing entities from an objective standpoint. The situation describes that state from the subjective standpoint through a set of relations and attributes. Thereby, it includes the internal and the external circumstances of an entity.

Example: The economic situation of a human being can be described only from a subjective standpoint. The assessment of whether a person is rich or poor is carried out by an observer. Various circumstances have to be considered, such as the average income of the population, or personal property. They form a relationship structure, which is used for evaluation.

Observation and Acting

How can such subjective formations arise from the objective reality? There must be a major cause of the objective-subjective dualism. One of the most obvious dynamics in this regard is the process of observing, concluding and acting. This process connects an observer and its subject of observation in a larger circularity. This corresponds to second-order cybernetics (Heylighen & Joslyn, 2001; von Foerster, 1992).

Observation

Often, observation is considered to be a discovery process that is non-intrusive in terms of the observed entities. But, some observations may have an implicit effect on the observed entities, for example in quantum mechanics, where each measurement determines the result of the electron spin. This effect is usually not desired by the observer and perceived as a disturbance (observer effect by de Bianchi (2013).

URANOS uses the term "observation" as an interaction between an observer and the observed entities. We do not exclude that this interaction might be intrusive.

Control Loop

An observer may also respond explicitly to perceived states. Therefore, he performs actions intending to modify the observed entities in a desired manner. This is called *control*. The associated process circuit is referred to as a *control loop*. It describes a continuous process for conducting and exerting power over another process.

Generally, a control system can be split into two subsystems: a *controlled system A* and a *controlling system B* (Figure 9). While A transforms inputs X_A into outputs Y_A, B observes some of A's outputs and compares internally

Figure 9. Control loop containing a controlling subsystem B and a controlled subsystem A (Inspired by Pangaro (1989)).

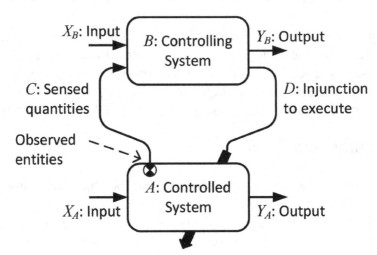

the observed quantities (C) with its desired goal. B then tries to balance the difference between observed quantities and the desired goal by directing A. In this context, B generates injunctions for execution (D). A has no choice and must obey the instructions given by B. B treats A like an "it". This kind of interaction between A and B is called "it-referenced" (Pangaro, 1989; Pask, 1975).

Example: When a person drives a car, he is monitoring the current situation on the street and steers, brakes or accelerates accordingly. This is referred to as intentional and goal-oriented acting, like keeping a speed limit or staying on the road. In this sense, the car is controlled by the driver. A process can control the speed as follows: The speed limit on the road is the given goal, with which the driver must comply. While the car (A) converts its fuel into motion, the driver (B) monitors the speed of the car (C), and compares this with the predetermined speed limit. Accordingly, the driver adapts the speed via the carburetor (D).

Perceptual Control Loop

To understand how subjectivity arises from the observation of entities, the control loop can be refined towards a sophisticated process called a *perceptual control loop* (Powers et al., 2008) (Figure 10).

Figure 10. Perceiving-acting process described as a perceptual control loop

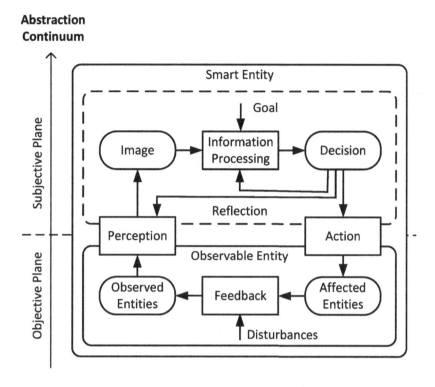

The process starts with the observation of entities. Preferably those which are relevant to the development of the system. This first step is called *perception*. It maps an external state to an internal representation, called an *image*. The mapping is relative to the observer's point of view and to his capabilities for constructing information (Bruegger, 2011; Hirsbrunner, Aguilar & Krone, 1994). This leads to individual (biased) perceptual inference. The observer experiences a subjective reality.

The images must be processed in order to understand what is happening, and to be able to respond appropriately. This information processing is responsible for creating models, acquiring knowledge, and finally could induce decisions about how to respond to the perceived situation. Decisions can be transformed into actions that affect some entities in the environment. The information processing is also accompanied by *reflection loops*. They enable the system to influence and to adapt the perception and decision-making functions.

A *feedback* function closes the control loop, whenever the set of affected and observed entities overlap each other. This function describes dynamics among observable entities including external influences that might be perceived as disturbances.

Awareness

Through the perceptual control loop, smart entities can perceive occurrences of significant objective states, called *events*. Further, it enables smart entities to become conscious of the event's existence, where being conscious is perceiving and paying attention to what is happening. This generates an emerging characteristic called *awareness*. It denotes the lowest stage of consciousness.

Definition [Awareness]: Awareness is the ability to perceive and be conscious of events.

Different kinds of awareness exist. For instance, a thermostat perceives a room temperature through a sensor. From its subjective standpoint, it is aware of the temperature. A human being can also be aware of very complex and abstract situations, like his economic situation, or climatic change.

Autopoietic System

Smart entities cover a spectrum of systems, from simple control systems like thermostats to complex living systems like human beings. Two major kinds are distinguished, which denominate the two ends of that spectrum: *allopoietic* and *autopoietic* systems (Heylighen & Joslyn, 2001; Maturana, Varela & Beer, 1980).

An allopoietic system corresponds to a smart entity, which is designed and maintained from the outside. It is typically an artificial or man-made system, like a smart phone or an industrial machine.

An autopoietic system is a smart entity that is able to maintain and to reproduce itself. It distinguishes itself from the outside world through operational closure. Its main goal is persistence by keeping its essential organization. All living systems belong to this category. Henceforth, the text refers to autopoietic systems.

Autopoiesis Loop

A autopoietic system exists on the objective and subjective planes. Each system keeps a subjective reality inside that reflects and abstracts the objective reality outside. In this dualism both realities influence each other.

The mutual influence of these two realities is a closed circuit, which is called the *autopoiesis loop*. It describes any kind of internalization (e.g. perception) and the resulting impacts on the objective reality (e.g. actions). Autopoiesis is also responsible for self-creation and self-maintaining, where it produces the boundaries of a system (Maturana et al., 1980) and distinguishes between the *exterior* and the *interior* of an autopoietic system (Luhmann, 2008).

Example: A living cell is an autopoietic system. It can internalize environmental states by building resonating internal structures. On one hand, these structures describe the cell's boundary to the external environment. But on the other hand, they also serve as a kind of a memory helping to remember and to react to recurring situations, an immanent network of potential relations (Schwarz, 2010). In this sense, the autopoiesis loop describes that internalization and self-producing process, and its influence back on the cell's environment.

Autopoietic Topology

All autopoietic systems maintain a set of internal entities representing their individual and subjective reality. Besides the abstraction of objective reality this set also encompasses other subjective constructs like goals, intentions and ideas. The way in which these internal entities are arranged is referred as an *autopoietic topology*. It is a part of the autopoietic system's identity, meaning that it is unique - "there are no doppelgangers" possible (Pask & de Zeeuw, 1992).

Example: A computer program can arrange its collected data in a semantic network, that can be used for decision-making. In this sense the organization of data in a semantic network can be seen as a topology. Since a computer system is an allopoietic system, its internal state can be duplicated. The programmer of the system behaves quite differently. His autopoietic topology is represented by his mind and as an autopoietic system his mind cannot be directly accessed and duplicated.

Reflection Loop

The autopoietic topology is maintained by the *reflection loop*. It includes all dynamics within an autopoietic topology, such as information processing, decision-making and acquiring knowledge. In one direction, perceived states are processed to make decisions. In the other direction, these decisions are reflected allowing smart entities to think about the essence of their autopoietic topology. This is an important process for the development of higher consciousness.

In summary, autopoiesis and reflection loops make up the dynamics of a smart entity (Figure 11).

THIRD-ORDER: ENACTIVE ENTITIES

Complex non-linear systems, like social and living systems, cannot be described solely by the objective-subjective dualism. Here, the way objective

Figure 11. Smart entity e_S made of the observed entity e_O and the autopoietic topology N, forming one system

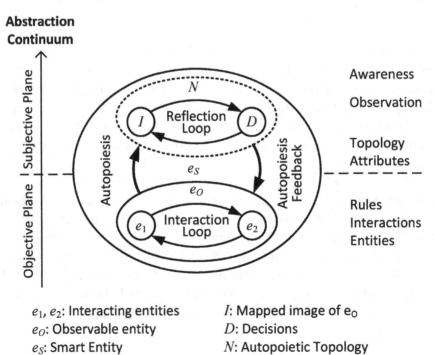

e_1, e_2: Interacting entities
e_O: Observable entity
e_S: Smart Entity

I: Mapped image of e_O
D: Decisions
N: Autopoietic Topology

reality and its subjective perception influence each other can no longer be described independently of one another, but must be considered and analyzed as a whole (Schwarz, 2002).

That induces another paradigm shift, which describes complex systems from the standpoint of holism. URANOS uses the holistic plane to describe aspects which emerge from holism.

Holistic Characteristics

An inseparable entity appears on the holistic plane representing the existential being. Entities that are characterized by such existential beings are called *enactive entities*. This includes all living systems such as humans, plants, and cells, as well as social systems, such as cultures and societies. The term "enaction" refers to the fact that cognition is the enactment of a reality and a mind based on a history of the variety of actions that a system performs (Varela, Thompson & Rosch, 1993, p. 9).

Enactive entities are characterized by three fundamental aspects:

1. **Consciousness:** Entities are aware of themselves and their surroundings. Consciousness is reinforced by the dynamics of an autopoietic system, in particular of its autopoiesis and reflection loops.
2. **Cre-Adaption:** Entities are able to adapt their behavior or create new behaviors. Cre-adaption is a capability that is enforced by consciousness and intentional acting. It respects the fact that an enactive entity is able to change its own rules (self-creation, autogenesis).
3. **Individuation:** Enactive entities are able to differentiate themselves from the environment. This process allows entities to become holistic beings, developing their own identity. It is accompanied by increasing cognitive capabilities (Jung, 1935).

Consciousness Complexity

On the holistic plane the objective and subjective realities are entangled and cannot be considered independently of each other. This is called *autogenetic entanglement* $\tilde{E}$, and thanks to it, enactive entities obtain consciousness (Schwarz, 2010). It is an epiphenomenon of the abstraction continuum. In a similar way K. Wilber (2007) stated, "every level of interior consciousness is accompanied by a level of exterior physical complexity. The greater the consciousness, the more complex the system housing it" (p. 57).

Consciousness is described through a spectrum, called *consciousness complexity*. It starts on the subjective plane where smart entities become aware of events. Here, awareness is a result of observation. Higher levels of consciousness arise from the cognitive abilities of enactive entities, due to the increasing autogenetic entanglement (Schwarz, 2010).

Example: A human being as a whole is influenced by its body and mind. For instance, positive thinking could encourage a person's health. But, the opposite is also true. Good health could have a positive influence on the person's mind. Through a reflective view onto this autogenetic entanglement of body and mind, a person can develop a consciousness, such as being self-aware of his personal health.

Cognition

Cognition is a broad term which is used here in the sense of gaining knowledge through interaction. It allows enactive entities to become aware of their surroundings or themselves, and to act intentionally (Varela et al., 1993). Cognition is not a fixed stage, but rather the capacity of an entity for cognitive development.

Example: Human mental development passes through several stages (Piaget, 1929). In the first stage of cognitive development a human child has not yet grasped what the distinction is between subject and object. The nature of thought and dreams remains unknown at this stage. The child has difficulties to describe the subjective nature of dreams. During cognitive development the child passes through several stages, where it gains the ability to think about itself and its environment.

Self-Awareness

An outstanding appearance of consciousness is *self-awareness*. It is the ability of an enactive entity to recognize itself as an individual distinct from the environment and other enactive entities. It differs from awareness in the following way: awareness is the ability to be conscious of a reality (objective, subjective or holistic), whereas self-awareness is the recognition that one is aware of that reality (Jabr, 2012). Not all enactive entities have this ability equally available. It is caused by general cognition, and often it overlaps with other cognitive stages.

Example: If a person looks at his foot, he sees a foot. If he knows that this foot is part of his body, this does not change the fact that he perceives the foot as a physical object. Only when he is also aware of the perception of his foot, combined with his connected feelings and thoughts, can one speak of self-awareness. Through it, he can learn on its basic nature, purpose and essence.

Towards Creativity and Empathy

Creativity and empathy are not stages on the spectrum of consciousness complexity, but emerge through higher consciousness and cognition. Both characteristics are important, because they have a great influence on the behavior of enactive entities. For example, if a society does not take creativity and empathy into account, it can easily lead to depression and finally to rebellion against the system.

Creativity and intuition allows the entity to find new ideas and to be innovative. Intuition refers to instinctively understanding, which is not solely based on reflective thinking. It happens through a process of consciousness, called *thought streams* (Gelernter, 1994).

Example: In dreams or day-dreams the mental focus of humans is lowered. In this state of low focus, thoughts are arbitrarily strung together generating thought streams. When the mental focus is back to the current situation of an entity (awake state) it happens that this thought stream becomes linked to that situation. This could induce new ideas and solutions and can be seen as an act of creativity (Gelernter, 1994).

Empathy allows an enactive entity to understand and feel the subjective realities of other entities, like emotions and thoughts. It is an important characteristic for social behavior and collaboration within groups of enactive entities. Self-awareness is a prerequisite for empathy. An entity must first be holistically aware of itself before it can put oneself in someone's shoes (Stein & Book, 2011). We use the term empathy in general, detached from neurological and emotional signals of biological creatures.

Example: J. Rozovsky analyzed high performing teams and showed that they do not necessarily consist of the right mix of expertise. Much more important is how they interact, appreciate each other's work and create an environment of psychological safety (Rozovsky, 2015). In this context, empathy helps to improve efficiency and performance in human teamwork. It underpins the collaboration and communication skills of a human team in order to solve conflicts and to maintain focus on their work (Luca & Tarricone, 2001). Therefore, when building teams or designing systems for teams, the holistic consideration of empathy is decisive for their future success.

Autogenetic System

The dynamics of an enactive entity are described as an *autogenetic system*. It's a system able to intervene in its own producing process and to determine and change its own laws. This is exactly what autonomy means (Schwarz, 2010).

In an autogenetic system the objective and subjective realities appear in the holistic plane in its existential dimension. The existence of observable entity e_O is denoted as $\tilde{e}_O$. Similarly, the existence of an autopoietic topology N is referred as $\tilde{N}$ (Figure 12).

Figure 12. Enactive entity e_E with consciousness as an epiphenomenon of the abstraction continuum

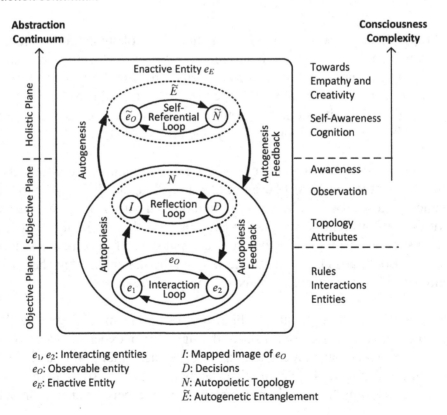

e_1, e_2: Interacting entities
e_O: Observable entity
e_E: Enactive Entity

I: Mapped image of e_O
D: Decisions
N: Autopoietic Topology
$\tilde{E}$: Autogenetic Entanglement

Autogenesis Loop

The autogenetic entanglement between $\tilde{e}_O$ and $\tilde{N}$ forms an inseparable whole, a holistic being. This being is not only affected by the lower autopoietic system, it also has an effect itself on the autopoietic system. This circularity between the autopoietic system and the holistic being is called an *autogenesis loop*. It is a process of cre-adaption and individuation that leads towards autonomy and self-determination (Schwarz, 2002).

Self-Referential Loop

The holistic being is maintained by a circularity on the holistic plane, called a *self-referential loop*. It represents the dynamics of the autogenetic entanglement, and is the main cause for higher consciousness. The stronger the entanglement, the higher the stages of consciousness that can be reached.

Autopoiesis and autogenesis ensure evolutionary change and contribute to the adaptivity and survival capacity of an enactive entity. The three maintaining loops on each plane, namely interaction, reflection and self-referential, contribute to the stability of the system (Schwarz, 2002). Together, these five loops characterize the dynamics of an enactive entity (Figure 12).

ENTITY COLLABORATION

URANOS considers all relevant entities that together describe a system. It is of particular interest how these entities collaborate, and what basic patterns of behavior and roles they have. Collaboration is defined as working together to pursue a common goal. There exist various forms of collaboration, such as cooperation and coordination.

Collaboration goes beyond simple interaction. Besides objective interactions it also requires an exchange about the essence of subjective reality, like models, intentions and goals. Through collaboration, enactive entities can develop a feeling of togetherness. In its perfection this provokes a symbiosis between systems (e.g. human-machine symbiosis). From our generic standpoint, symbiosis is defined as a *collaborative entanglement* between participating entities.

Goal-Directness

Whether as an autonomous entity or as a collective, smart entities can pursue goals to oppose changes in the environment and to adapt accordingly. The term "goal" describes a desired state of smart entities. The entity attempts to compensate for any deviations in order to pursue its goal. Thus, the goal can be seen as a future stable state (equilibrium).

The primary goal of autopoietic systems is survival, which is the retention of the most vital and identity-forming structures (Goldstein, 1988; Heylighen & Joslyn, 2001). Other goals may be subordinated to that primary goal. For example, finding food is a subsidiary goal for living systems, but it contributes to the primary goal of survival. For allopoietic systems, primary goals are preset by their designers, so that they are able to tend to a stable equilibrium. For instance, the primary goal of a robot is to contribute to a preset goal of its designer, like supporting a manufacturing process, or searching for mines.

Goal-directness is a characteristic of an entity. It describes how an entity pursues goals. It takes beliefs, motives and decision-making into account.

Motives

Smart entities have an internal drive for achieving their goals. This drive causes entities to act. This is called a *motive* for the entity's activity (Kuutti, 1995).

Definition [Motive]: The entity's urge causing the entity to act in a certain way is called motive.

Motives cannot be considered independently of perception and beliefs. They are based on fundamental beliefs, which encompass reasoning about the objective reality and how this reality can be influenced.

The motive drives the decision-making process. It's necessary to know the motive of an entity in order to understand its behavior. Knowing the entity's motive, its behavior becomes more predictable. In collaboration, the motives of each participating entity decide how effectively common goals can be pursued together.

Strategy

Smart entities are able to work out a set of rules, which they will apply in upcoming situations. This set describes the entity's strategy to reach goals.

Definition [Strategy]: The set of rules applicable in the future to reach a goal is called strategy.

Example: The motive of a predator is to feed its offspring, so that the breed survives. Therefore, he develops a strategy for how he can most easily hunt his prey. It is a set of rules that help him to adapt his behavior in situations more efficiently. Among primitive predators these rules are produced mainly by instinct. Hunters with higher consciousness can devise an individual plan.

Conversation

It is essential for collaboration that smart entities can exchange their individual understanding of reality, their goals and intentions. Generally, this is done by communication, an interaction that takes place between entities on the subjective plane. Thus, in the case of allopoietic systems, one can access the entire subjective content. For example, a person can access the entire memory content of a computer. On the other hand, it is not possible to directly access the subjective content of an autopoietic system, due to its operational closure. Here, a more comprehensive process is needed to exchange subjective constructs, called *conversation*. It describes a complex interaction between smart entities, which mainly depends on one entity's interpretation of the other's behavior (Pask, 1975; Pangaro, 1989).

Conversation Process

Conversation includes at least two entities wherein both entities can take the role of a knowledge provider or the role of a knowledge recipient. While conversing, the assignment of these roles can dynamically change depending on the subject of discussion.

Let's assume that an entity *B* (knowledge provider) explains some novel concepts to an entity *A* (knowledge recipient). *B* will constantly check if it appears that *A* has understood. If *B* still finds marginal differences he might use other examples to illustrate what he meant. This is repeated until the conversation process may end in a mutual agreement of understanding, or is aborted by one of the participants. In the first case it leads to the construction of shared knowledge between the participating entities allowing them to negotiate about goals and to agree (or disagree) upon a common understanding of concepts (Dubberly & Pangaro, 2009). And in the second case, the exchange will be stopped, which also leads to a termination of the collaboration.

Example: Some children are playing outside in the snow. Someone has the idea to build an igloo together. Before this project can be started, the others need to be convinced that this is the right goal. When a child shares that goal, then a foundation has been laid for collaboration. But it may also be that some do not see the meaning or prefer to do something else. In this case no collaboration occurs.

The Role of Language

Smart entities must share a common conversation language in order to share their subjective reality. This allows them to express and describe topic content, like building an igloo. A language refers to any means for expressing subjective aspects like models, intentions or goals. The embodiment of language might be speech, body language, communication over pheromones or even actions.

A conversation is always topic related. Everything an entity undertakes to share a topic i with others is based on topic relations R_i which are embodied in a conversation language. R_i contains entities explaining, describing or questioning a topic i (Pask, 1975).

Example: The topic of the children is "building an igloo". For instance, "how can I build an igloo?" or "an igloo is made of snow and ice" are topic relations, that are used in their conversation language. Assuming that each child speaks their own spoken language, these relations can be embodied in a body language instead. A child A might show using gestures that it does not know how to build an igloo. Another child B responds to these gestures, and creates an example of the first block of snow. This action is perceived by A and may lead to understanding or further questions.

Levels

In a conversation, there are different communication levels. The more levels there are, the more flexibly and extensively a topic can be mediated. Typically, conversation requires at least two levels (Figure 13): L_0 is called the *method level*, which exposes the "how". It deals with A's reinterpretation of modeling instructions delivered by B. The second level, L_1, is called the *goal level*. It provides the explanation of the model itself. This corresponds to the "why" (Pask, 1975).

Figure 13. Conversation model from Pask (1975) which consists of at least the two levels to exchange methods and goals

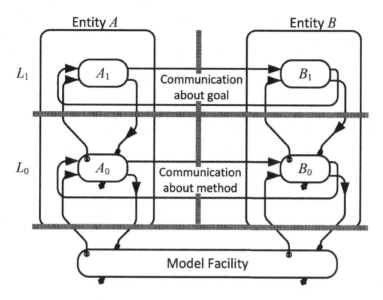

Example: It is insufficient to convey only the "how". The children who see no point in building an igloo, cannot be convinced with "how do I build an igloo". Likewise, it is also insufficient to provide only the "why". At this level, the knowledge of how to build an igloo cannot be spread. Only through the interplay of these two levels is knowledge shared, promoting a common understanding in the group.

These two levels form the basic framework for conversation. At each level there is a process that can exploit the information provided. The processes A_0 and B_0 handle the modeling instructions, where A_1 and B_1 handle the explanations. Each participant entertains a hypothesis about how to model a topic relation R_i. The model is generated out of a repertoire of procedures able to process R_i (e.g. A_0 or B_0). This forms the entity's own subjective intention of R_i. Within the bounds of a *modeling facility*, in a universe of the participant's own choice, he can instantiate and verify or deny the model. The conversation stops on R_i once the models of A and B match. A and B reach a mutual agreement of understanding of the topic relation R_i. The conversation may proceed on another topic relation.

Symbiosis

The collaboration and unity of the entities is manifested by circularities at each abstraction plane. Unlike control loops, entities and processes are not controlled by these interactions. They allow them to communicate with each other on the same level. This kind of interaction between *A* and *B* is called "I/You-referenced" because entities participate equally in that interaction (Pangaro, 1989). The result is a collaborative entanglement between the participating entities, called symbiosis (Figure 14). In this sense, symbiosis is a complex interaction between entities, which results in a mutual benefit for all of them (Paracer & Ahmadjian, 2000).

In contrast to mutualism in biology, the term "symbiosis" can also refer here to mutually beneficial interactions between entities of the same species. For example, if two people need each other so that they can pursue their common goal, then a symbiosis happens.

Figure 14. Collaborative entanglement between enactive entities A and B through the interaction loop, conversation loop and social cohesion loop

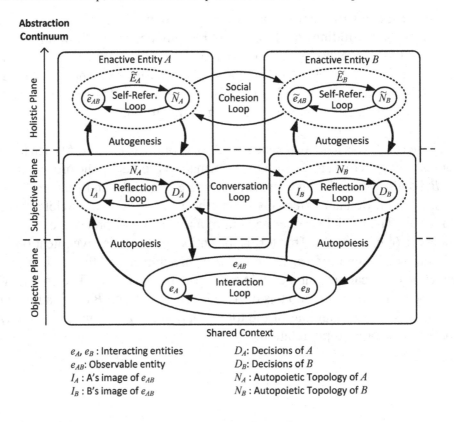

e_A, e_B : Interacting entities D_A: Decisions of A
e_{AB}: Observable entity D_B: Decisions of B
I_A : A's image of e_{AB} N_A : Autopoietic Topology of A
I_B : B's image of e_{AB} N_B : Autopoietic Topology of B

First-Order Symbiosis

Within the objective plane, entities take part in an interaction-loop expressing an objective interaction among them. At this stage, symbiosis is manifested in its weakest form, called *first-order symbiosis*. This kind of symbiosis is described from a purely objective standpoint.

Example: Any chemical compound is a first-order symbiosis. For instance, hydrogen and oxygen atoms enter into a chemical reaction process. In the resulting chemical compound two hydrogen atoms share their electrons with one oxygen atom (H_2O). Together, they form a symbiosis, which produces new chemical properties as a whole. The individual atoms benefit from that symbiosis, since their energy levels become more stable.

Second-Order Symbiosis

Smart entities are connected to each other on both objective and subjective planes. The circularity on the subjective plane is called a *conversation loop*. It allows smart entities to exchange their subjective realities with each other. This loop facilitates smart entities' acquisition of new knowledge and insights, which they haven't experienced themselves.

The conversation loop is a fundamental feature for smart entities. Only in this way can they reach a mutual agreement on understanding, which is a prerequisite for any collaboration. The result is a *second-order symbiosis*, where smart entities become dependent on their shared objective and subjective realities. An individual contemplation of their activities and their beliefs is no longer possible. Rather, the collective must now be taken into account.

Example: Human-machine symbiosis belongs to second-order symbiosis. Here humans and machines enter into a closed conversation loop that allows them to share their knowledge and models. Current representatives of human-machine symbiosis are the Internet and smart phones. Human activities today depend on these technologies to a high degree.

Third-Order Symbiosis

Between enactive entities there exists a third loop on the holistic plane allowing them to be part of a social group. This loop is called the *social cohesion loop*. It is a prerequisite for togetherness and collectiveness.

If enactive entities are interconnected through all three loops, then a *third-order symbiosis* arises. From the holistic standpoint, the participating entities form a new wholeness. They can no longer be decoupled from each other without changing their nature and behavior.

Example: The third-order symbiosis is typical for biological and sociological symbiosis. Human societies are formed by third-order symbiosis. It allows human beings to be part of a social group. In extreme cases it is impossible for human beings to quit that group afterwards.

SYSTEM DEVELOPMENT

One of the key questions is how complex entities could arise in the universe over time. We intend to describe the process leading to complexity, called *system development*. Through this process, systems can grow or shrink in complexity. Accordingly, new dynamics and systemic aspects could emerge or disappear on the different abstraction planes (Figure 15).

Stages of System Development

A system passes through several stages in its development. These stages are characterized by feedback loops, namely reinforcing or dampening feedback. Because several feedback loops may overlap each other, the appropriate effect can vary in different intensities. In fact, the transitions leading to different stages are blurred. Therefore, we describe them on a spectrum called the

Figure 15. Evolution and involution of system's complexity

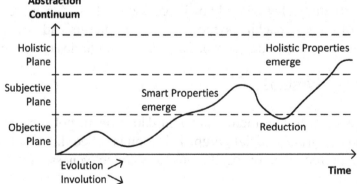

Figure 16. Spectrum of development in correlation with the degree of dampening and reinforcing effects

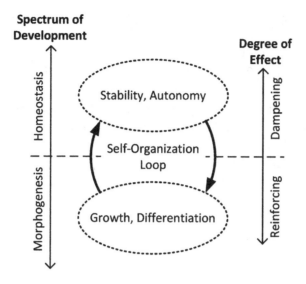

spectrum of development (Figure 16). It is split into two planes, which are distinguished by the development tendency they represent: morphogenesis and homeostasis.

Morphogenesis

The first plane is called *morphogenesis*. It describes stages of development that are characterized by growth and differentiation. Here the system is mainly affected by reinforcing feedbacks, where changes are amplified. The results are new structures, processes and organizations appearing across the entire system.

Example: The embryonic stage of a human being is characterized by morphogenesis. Here, cells start to differentiate themselves building new structures like bones, organs and the brain. Besides the outweighed reinforcing feedback loops there are also some dampening feedback loops that appear. The embryo starts to develop its own blood pressure, or starts to control its body temperature.

Homeostasis

The second plane is called *homeostasis*. Dampening feedback loops prevail in the system development at this stage. This promotes order, stability and constancy in the system.

As complexity increases new dynamics and systemic aspects could emerge in homeostasis. In the case of an enactive entity, the autogenetic entanglement starts to influence the autopoietic system through the autogenesis loop. This means that the system could start developing its cognitive capabilities, like self-awareness. From now on, the autogenetic system can only be understood as a whole. In its further development, the stability is increased. For enactive entities in particular, this means that they tend towards autonomy.

Example: A human being goes through homeostasis for becoming independent of his parents. Through increasing cognitive abilities, a human being starts to decide more independently and act more autonomously (Piaget, 1929).

Driving Forces

There exist two forces driving the evolution of a system. One, called *entropic drift*, leads to disorder and change (Schwarz, 2002). The other, called *self-organization*, leads to order and stability. The interplay of these two forces is referred to as the *self-organization loop* (Figure 16).

These forces are not globally acting forces, but rather force fields acting differently in each subsystem. Thus, for example, in some subsystems the entropic drift might be the dominant force, where in other subsystems it might be the self-organization.

Entropic Drift

The major force is called *entropic drift*. It is responsible for fluctuations, non-deterministic and random events that happen within a system or its environment. They cause an increase in entropy. From the subjective standpoint such events are often perceived by observers as disturbances or noise.

Together with reinforcing feedback loops small fluctuations and inclinations are amplified. This could lead to a discontinuity of the system behavior and could drive the system far from its stability (equilibrium) (Schwarz, 2002; Yolles, 2006). Entropic drift is crucial, as it brings the system away from its stability, allowing it to find new ways of development. It could catapult the system towards a higher level of development (evolution) or towards degeneration (involution).

Example: A pendulum, which remains in its rest position, can be regarded as a system in equilibrium. The pendulum cannot move from this position on its own. It requires action from the outside, such as an interaction with a person who makes the pendulum move. From the perspective of the pendulum, this can be seen as a disturbance, which has an abrupt impact on the overall system.

Self-Organization

Suppose that a system (or a subsystem) enters a state of the attractor E_A (equilibrium), then it cannot reach any states outside the attractor anymore. The uncertainty of which state the system is in, has been decreased. This spontaneous reduction of entropy corresponds to the increase of order, and denotes *self-organization* (Heylighen & Joslyn, 2001).

In general, self-organizing brings greater stability and autonomy to the system, meaning it drives the system towards an equilibrium. The force to self-organize is responsible for the system tending towards homeostasis.

But it could happen that a system ends at some stage of development, without reaching its optimal stability. Entropic drift can cause the system to leave this "local" stable stage, driving the self-organization further towards more stable and autonomous stages, and causing self-organizing processes to speed up. This principle is also called *order from noise* (von Foerster, 2003).

TOWARDS N-TH ORDER SYSTEMS

With holism, we did not reach a final standpoint which explains all aspects of a system. Through paradigm shifts new epistemological standpoints will be developed in the future describing complex systems even more comprehensively. Our generic model is not limited to third-order systems. We intend to show how URANOS can be extended to make new epistemological standpoints accessible for system design.

Assume that through a paradigm shift a new epistemological standpoint is developed, from which new systemic aspects are discovered. The comprehensive system model, which includes the existing and new aspects, leads to a higher ordered system. A new systemic order is added to the model similarly

Figure 17. Paradigm shift leading to a new standpoint and finally to an n-th order system that encapsulates the lower systemic orders

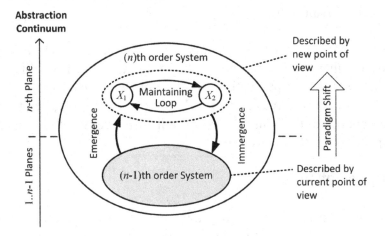

as it has been shown for first-, second- and third-order. In general, a new system of *n*-th order encapsulates the existing system of (*n*-1)-th order, and extends it with the new aspects discovered from the *n*-th standpoint (Figure 17).

The dynamics between the emerging aspects X_1 and X_2 are described by a loop maintaining the system at the *n*-th abstraction plane. The new epistemological standpoint also prescribes a process of emergence and immergence, called the *emergence/immergence loop*. It describes the mutual influence between the (*n*-1)-th ordered systems and the emerging dynamics on the *n*-th abstraction plane.

Systemic Order vs. Layers

A new systemic order describes novel characteristics and aspects that are very difficult to explain without that new order. New orders help to describe a system in a more simple way. In terms of cybernetic systems M. Yolles and G. Fink (2014) state "higher cybernetic order facilitates simpler modelling under increasing complexity. Thus, while the models become more complex with increasing order, they are simpler relative to increasing complexity. Each higher order has a potential to create a family of paradigms through new ways of seeing" (p. 2).

In contrast to systemic order, layering is used primarily in man-made systems. Here it does not bring new systemic aspects. Nor does it need a compelling paradigm shift to add new layers. It is a purely architectural process to make a system more manageable and maintainable for human designers (Figure 18).

Figure 18. The difference between systemic orders and system layers

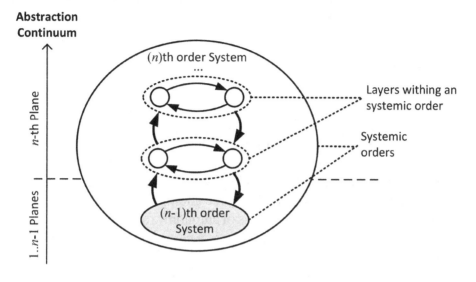

Holon: Possible Fourth-Order?

There are certain trends and initiatives that might lead towards fourth-order systems. A promising approach is the concept of the *holon*. Still, many open questions remain that we could not answer in depth in our work.

Epistemological Standpoint

The term *holon* refers to an entity that is a wholeness, but also a part of another whole at the same time. The resulting topology is called a *holarchy* (Koestler, 1976).

The epistemological standpoint of *holonism* states that reality is made of holons (whole/parts) only. From that standpoint there is no such thing as complete autonomy. As mentioned by K. Wilber (1995) "as a whole, a holon possesses a degree of autonomy, expressed in its identifying and enduring pattern, its self-preservation...As a part, however, every holon - the autonomy of every holon - is subjected to larger forces and systems of which it is merely a component" (p. 106f).

Example: Humans are not standalone organisms, but embedded in a socio-cultural environment. Humans as a whole can operate autonomously to some extent. But because human beings are affected by the socio-cultural environment, they can hardly be seen as completely autonomous beings. They are parts of social groups, which constitute more comprehensive wholes.

Holonic System

URANOS implicitly follows the principle of holonism. An enactive entity is a whole, but it is also an entity in the objective plane interacting with other entities. With the paradigm shift of holons this circumstance can be explicitly described on an additional abstraction plane, called the *holonic plane*. Systems that encompass the holonic plane are referred to as *holonic systems*.

There are two opposed forces. One force attempts to preserve the aspects of wholeness by promoting the process of autonomy (autogenesis). The other force reinforces the aspect that the holon is a part of higher holons. There is a maintaining loop, which is responsible for balancing this kind of dynamics between the whole and the part. Finally, there must also be an emergence/immergence loop connecting the autogenetic system with the dynamics between whole and part. However, this loop still raises many open questions that are not answered in this book.

Open Questions

With regard to the dynamics of the fourth-order there are several open questions. These issues could not be clarified or explored as part of this research, because fundamental knowledge is still lacking in this domain. The corresponding discussion needs to be done first, regardless of our model. The key issues are:

1. What are the characteristics of the new emergence/immergence loop? And how does it influence the holon and its lower-ordered autogenetic system?
2. What is the maintaining loop about? Is it purely balancing the whole/part characteristic? Or is it something more like a self-definition loop, as proposed by M. Yolles and G. Fink (2014)?
3. How does fourth-order cybernetics correspond to holons and holarchy (Attainable Utopias, 2016)?

SUMMARY

The model of URANOS is presented as a generic system model. It intends to give a deeper insight into the dynamics and the organization of complex non-linear systems, such as living systems. The model shows how stable complex systems can evolutionarily develop and how they can collaborate in a mutually beneficial manner. The generic approach is mainly based on two insights. Firstly, various epistemological standpoints are needed to explain the totality of a system. The model consists of three epistemological standpoints: objectivism, subjectivism and holism. Secondly, all the characteristics and classifications are based on the principle of a spectrum. There are no clear boundaries, and in the best case there is only a subjective mapping possible. The main spectrum of URANOS is the abstraction continuum, which describes the level of abstraction of all system constructs. Concerning the epistemological standpoints, the abstraction continuum is divided into three planes: objective, subjective and holistic.

Various systemic orders can be described by the model. First-order systems are denoted as observable entities. They describe well bounded systems that are observable from the outside. Such systems are expressed by the objective standpoint introducing two basic constructs: entities and interaction. Smart entities are second-order systems. At this level there exists a dualism between objectivity and subjectivity. The observer is included in a larger circularity leading to new aspects like awareness. As third-order systems, enactive entities describe holistic beings that cannot be understood solely by the study of their components. They must be considered as a whole. Here the objective-subjective dualism disappears in an autogenetic entanglement. New system characteristics emerge, like consciousness, cre-adaption and individuation.

If two or more entities work together, this leads to a symbiosis. The model describes symbiosis as a collaborative entanglement between two or more entities pursuing a common goal, which generates a mutual benefit. On each abstraction plane there exists a connecting loop that maintains the symbiosis. On the objective plane entities are coupled through interaction loops, denoting concrete interaction between them. On the subjective plane a conversation loop enables the entities to exchange constructs of their subjective realities, like ideas, models and goals. The social cohesion loop connects exclusively enactive entities on their holistic planes. It allows them to enter into a social group and to be part of it.

The model expresses the evolution of complex systems through development stages and driving forces. There are two opposing forces that affect the development: the urge for self-organization, which leads to order and structure in the system; and entropic drift, which provokes disorder and change.

URANOS is flexible in terms of extensibility through new systemic orders. As a possible extension the concept of holon is presented, an entity which is simultaneously both a wholeness and part of a larger wholeness. This rises several open questions about holonic dynamics. Further research is needed on that epistemological standpoint, before our model can be extended in this direction.

REFERENCES

Attainable Utopias. (2016, June 28). *Fourth-order cybernetics*. Retrieved from http://www.attainable-utopias.com/tiki/FourthOrderCybernetics

Bruegger, P. (2011). *uMove: a wholistic framework to design and implement ubiquitous computing systems supporting user's activity and situation* (Doctoral dissertation). Retrieved from réro Doc. (R006095784)

Cram101 Textbook Reviews. (Ed.). (2013). *e-Study Guide for Ethics: Theory and Contemporary Issues, textbook y Barbara MacKinnon: Philosophy, Ethics*. Cram101.

Crane, T. (2001). The Significance of Emergence. In B. Loewer & G. Gillett (Eds.), *Physicalism and its Discontents* (pp. 207–224). Cambridge, UK: Cambridge University Press. doi:10.1017/CBO9780511570797.011

Darwin, C. (1859). *On the Origin of Species by Means of Natural Selection*. London, UK: John Murray.

de Bianchi, S. M. (2013). The Observer Effect. *Foundations of Science, 18*(2), 213-243.

Dobzhansky, T. G. (1937). *Genetics and the Origin of Species*. New York, NY: Columbia University Press.

Dubberly, H., & Pangaro, P. (2009). On Modeling - What is conversation, and how can we design for it? *Interaction, 16*(4), 22–28. doi:10.1145/1551986.1551991

Forrester, J. W. (1969). *Principles of Systems*. Cambridge, MA: Wright-Allen Press Inc.

Freud, S. (1993). The Psychical Apparatus and the Theory of Instincts. In C. Lemert (Ed.), *Social Theory. The Multicultural and Classic Readings* (pp. 137–141). Westview Press.

Gelernter, D. H. (1994). *The Muse in the Machine: Computerizing the Poetry of Human Thought.* New York, NY: The Free Press.

Goldstein, J. (1988). A far-from-Equilibrium Systems Approach to Resistance to Change. *Organizational Dynamics, 17*(2), 16–26. doi:10.1016/0090-2616(88)90016-2

Heylighen, F., & Joslyn, C. (2001). Cybernetics and Second-Order Cybernetics. In R. A. Meyers (Ed.), *Encyclopedia of Physical Science & Technology* (pp. 155–170). New York, NY: Academic Press.

Hirsbrunner, B., Aguilar, M., & Krone, O. (1994). CoLa: A Coordination Language for Massive Parallelism. In *Proceedings ACM Symposium on Principles of Distributed Computing (PODC).* New York, NY: ACM. doi:10.1145/197917.198156

Jabr, F. (2012). Self-Awareness with a Simple Brain. *Scientific American Mind, 23*, 28–29.

Jung, C. G. (1935). *Die Beziehungen zwischen dem Ich und dem Unbewussten.* Zurich, Switzerland: Rascher.

Kelber, K. (1999). Triops cancriformis (Crustacea, Notostraca): Ein bemerkenswertes Fossil aus der Trias Mitteleuropas. In N. Hauschke & V. Wilde (Eds.), *Trias-Eine ganz andere Welt* (Vol. 3, pp. 383–394). München, Germany: Verlag Dr. Friedrich Pfeil.

Koestler, A. (1967). *The Ghost in the Machine.* London, UK: Hutchinson.

Kuutti, K. (1995). Activity Theory as a potential framework for human-computer interaction research. In B. A. Nardi (Ed.), *Context and Consciousness: Activity Theory and Human Computer Interaction* (pp. 17–44). Cambridge, MA: MIT-Press.

Luca, J., & Tarricone, P. (2001). Does Emotional Intelligence Affect Successful Teamwork? *Meeting at the Crossroads.Proceedings of the 18th Annual Conference of the Australasian Society for Computers in Learning in Tertiary Education (ASCILITE 2001).*

Luhmann, N. (2008). *Soziologische Aufklärung 6 - Die Soziologie und der Mensch* (3rd ed.). VS Verlag für Sozialwissenschaften.

Maturana, H. R., Varela, F. J., & Beer, S. (1980). *Autopoiesis and Cognition: The Realization of the Living* (1st ed.). Springer. doi:10.1007/978-94-009-8947-4

Mendel, G. (1866). Versuche über Pflanzenhybriden. *Verhandlungen des naturforschenden Vereines in Brünn, 4*, 3-47.

Pangaro, P. (1989). *The Architecture of Conversation Theory*. Retrieved from http://www.pangaro.com/L1L0/ArchCTBriefly2b.htm

Paracer, S., & Ahmadjian, V. (2000). *Symbiosis: An Introduction to Biological Associations* (2nd ed.). New York, NY: Oxford University Press.

Pask, G. (1975). *Conversation, Cognition and Learning: A Cybernetic Theory and Methodology*. New York, NY: Elsevier Publishing Company.

Pask, G., & de Zeeuw, G. (1992). *Interactions of Actors, Theory and some Applications* (unpublished). Retrieved from http://www.cybsoc.org/PasksIAT.PDF

Piaget, J. (1929). *The Child's Conception of the World*. London, UK: Routledge & K. Paul Ltd.

Powers, W. T., Abbott, B., Carey, T. A., Goldstein, D. M., Mansell, W., Marken, R. S., & Taylor, M. et al. (2008). Perceptual Control Theory - A Model for Understanding the Mechanisms and Phenomena of Control. In D. Forssell (Ed.), *Perceptual Control Theory: Science & Applications: A Book of Readings* (pp. 18–34). Living Control Systems Publishing.

Rand, A. (1990). *Introduction to Objectivist Epistemology*. New York: New American Library.

Renevey, C., Aguilar, M., Hirsbrunner, B., & Krone, O. (1995a). *COLA: Yet Another Coordination Language. Workshop Parallel-Algorithmen*. Postdam, Germany: Rechnerstrukturen und-Systemsoftware.

Ricketts, T., & Levine, J. (1996). Logic and Truth in Frege. *Aristotelian Society Supplementary, 70*(1), 121–175. doi:10.1093/aristoteliansupp/70.1.121

Rozovsky, J. (2015). *The five keys to a successful Google team*. Retrieved from https://rework.withgoogle.com/blog/five-keys-to-a-successful-google-team/

Schwarz, E. (2002). Can Real Life Complex Systems Be Interpreted with the Usual Dualist Physicalist Epistemology - Or is a Holistic Approach Necessary? *Proceedings of the fifth European Systems Science Congress, 2*, 1-9.

Schwarz, E., & Dubois, D. M. (2010). On the Nature of Consciousness - On Consciousness in Nature. *AIP Conference Proceedings*, *1303*, 334–342. doi:10.1063/1.3527171

Stein, S. J., & Book, H. E. (2011). *The EQ Edge: Emotional Intelligence and Your Success*. Mississauga, ON, Canada: John Wiley & Sons Canada, Ltd.

Varela, F. J., Thompson, E., & Rosch, E. (1993). *The Embodied Mind: Cognitive Science and Human Experience*. Cambridge, MA: The MIT Press.

Vester, F. (1976). Studiengruppe Biologie und Umwelt & Regionale Planungsgemeinschaft Untermain.Ballungsgebiete in der Krise: eine Anleitung zum Verstehen und Planen menschlicher Lebensräume mit Hilfe der Biokybernetik. Stuttgart, Germany: Deutsche Verlags-Anstalt.

von Bertalanffy, L. (1968). *General System Theory: Foundations, Development, Applications*. New York, NY: George Braziller Inc.

von Foerster, H. (1992). Ethics and Second Order Cybernetics. *Cybernetics & Human Knowing*, *1*(1), 9–19.

von Foerster, H. (2003). *On Self-Organizing Systems and Their Environments. In Understanding Understanding: Essays on Cybernetics and Cognition* (pp. 1–19). New York, NY: Springer. doi:10.1007/0-387-21722-3_1

Wilber, K. (1995). *Sex, Ecology, Spirituality: The Spirit of Evolution*. Boston, MA: Shambhala Publications.

Wilber, K. (2007). *The Integral Vision: A Very Short Introduction to the Revolutionary Integral Approach to Life, God, the Universe, and Everything*. Boston, MA: Shambhala Publications.

Yolles, M., & Fink, G. (2014). *Generic Agency Theory, Cybernetic Orders and New Paradigms*. Retrieved from http://papers.ssrn.com/sol3/papers.cfm?abstract_id=2463270

ENDNOTE

[1]   Reinforcing feedback is referred in Forrester (1969) as "positive feedback"; and dampening feedback as "negative feedback".

Chapter 3
Model Instantiations

ABSTRACT

In three specific model instantiations, this chapter demonstrates how URANOS can be applied to other research domains. The first instantiation, referred to as the body-mind continuum, addresses humans as holistic and spiritual beings embedded in their natural, informational and socio-cultural environments. The second instantiation provides a framework for integral thinking and designing based on the AQAL-model from K. Wilber (2007). The third instantiation addresses holistic and cognitive coordination processes in the context of multi-agent and cyber-physical systems. These three instantiations together build the core of our human-centered modeling approach. Each of them holds our generic system model at its core, but at the same time has its own specific extensions.

INTRODUCTION

We aim to instantiate URANOS for three distinct but related models, which together build the core for human-centered systems. These models are described in depth in this chapter. On the one hand, they handle human beings and technical systems, and on the other hand, they promote holistic approaches for a better understanding of complex systems. The new findings, that URANOS contributes to modeling are emphasized.

The first model deals with living systems, especially human beings. The comprehension of human beings is fundamental for human-centered systems. From a holistic perspective, people can be regarded as bodies with a

DOI: 10.4018/978-1-5225-1888-4.ch003

mind, but also as spiritual beings. They are also not completely autonomous systems, but must be considered in the larger context of their environments. This model illustrates how body, mind and spirit are interrelated and interact with other humans and the environment.

The second model is concerned with integral thinking. It's a holistic approach that aims to integrate as many perspectives as possible to obtain a comprehensive picture of a complex system. The AQAL-model is chosen as an instantiation of URANOS. Our approach is to extend it with the perspective of system dynamics. This allows a deeper understanding of how complex systems behave, and how realities and their entities influence each other.

Finally, the third model outlines the coordinative aspects of allopoietic and computerized systems, such as multi-agent and cyber physical-systems. The model provides a deeper insight into coordination and dynamics within these systems. Once human beings and allopoietic systems enter into a symbiosis, a new high level coordination aspect emerges, called cognitive coordination. Coordination processes emerge at this level due to the cognitive and empathic capabilities of human beings.

Section "Body-Mind Continuum of Human Beings" presents an instantiation of living systems, in particular a model for human beings. We call this model the *body-mind continuum* expressing the fuzziness between body, mind and spirit. The second instantiation in section "Integral Thinking" addresses integral thinking and the AQAL model. Section "Coordination Model" provides a coordination model, designated for technical systems like multi-agent and cyber-physical systems. Finally, section "Conclusion" concludes the instantiation of URANOS.

BODY-MIND CONTINUUM OF HUMAN BEINGS

Living systems, and human beings in particular, are among the most complex systems which are known to us. We consider such systems as holistic, because they cannot solely be described by their parts, but must be also considered as wholes.

This section first addresses the mind-body problem, where some of the philosophical and epistemological key points have to be clarified. Then, we turn to the actual model for human beings, called the *body-mind continuum*. It expresses the fuzziness between body, mind and spirit. In particular, the model describes the relationships and dynamics between body, mind and spirit. Human beings can interact with each other and are embedded in an environment. Therefore, this section also addresses human interactions within an environment, how this affects the essence of human beings, and what potentials it brings to them.

The Mind-Body Problem

The body-mind continuum is accompanied by challenging questions that go far beyond biological research. One of the most fundamental discussions concerns the way body and mind are interrelated and influence each other. This problem is known as the *mind-body problem*[1]. Various research domains deal with this issue, such as philosophy, cybernetics and computer science. To date, no conclusive arguments or theories have been formulated for tackling this problem.

Cartesian Dualism

The mind-body problem was formulated by R. Descartes in the 17th century. From his standpoint, body and mind are distinct kinds of substances. The body (*res extensa*) refers to an extended physical substance, which is not capable of feeling or thinking. On the other hand, the mind (*res cogitans*) refers to an unextended substance that feels and thinks (Descartes, 1968).

This standpoint leads to a dualism, an epistemological perspective separating mental and physical entities. This dualism raises new questions rather than solving the problem. For instance, it is unclear how physical causes may bring about mental effects and vice versa. Is there a mental causation at all, or are mental states at the end only of a physical nature?

Mindbodies

The mind-body problem is trapped in the thought of dualism. We state that this issue cannot be solved, but it can be bypassed through a different approach. In eastern philosophies, like Buddhism and Hinduism, the psychological aspects (*nāma*) and physical body (*rūpa*) are mutually dependent, and form an inseparable being. The term *nāmarūpa* is used here referring to a human being, an identity of a human (Davids, Stede & Pâli Text Society, 1921).

From our standpoint, body and mind are just two different aspects of the same thing. The body comprises physical, chemical and neural states and interactions. But body is also "mind" embodying all mental states and processes. And vice versa. Living systems per se are "mindbodies", they are minds and bodies at once, inseparable in every aspect (Poteat, 1985). In other words, body and mind are two coexisting aspects describing a human being on different abstraction planes.

The dualistic mind-body problem can be circumvented by considering human beings as a whole. It is not possible to explain or solve this problem in depth. But, on the assumption that emergence/immergence loops exist, we are able to instantiate URANOS for human beings. Here, their existence appears on the holistic plane describing the inseparable entanglement of body and mind.

Human Being

Human beings are enactive entities for two reasons: (1) body and mind are entangled and form an autogenetic system (cf. section "Autogenetic System" in chapter "URANOS: A Generic System Model"); and as a consequence (2) they fulfill the three characteristics of enactive entities, namely consciousness, cre-adaption and individuation.

Following an integral thinking perspective (Wilber, 2007; Schwarz, 2010), they are defined in terms of three subsystems, each one belonging to an abstraction plane: body, mind and spirit (Figure 1).

Body

From the objective standpoint the body is seen as a bio-mechanical machine made of physical entities, like molecules, genes, cells and organs. It is maintained by many internal circuits which, for instance, control the body temperature, supply energy, or manage the defense against virus attacks.

One can argue that the body is an operationally closed system. The human skin therefore denotes the system border. The internal entities operate autonomously and are independent from the environment. However, there is no clear boundary between a human and his environment. Entities that form this boundary may belong to the body or the environment depending on the point of view. In addition, there are interactions that overcome this border, such as energy consumption or breathing. In summary, the body is a partially and operationally closed system with a fuzzy system boundary.

Mind

The mind is made of mental entities and of processes building an autopoietic topology. Images, thoughts and beliefs build models trying to express the objective reality as accurately as possible. These models are the key to how

Figure 1. Model of human beings as enactive entities made of a physical body, a mind as an autopoietic topology, and a spirit as a strong entanglement of body and mind

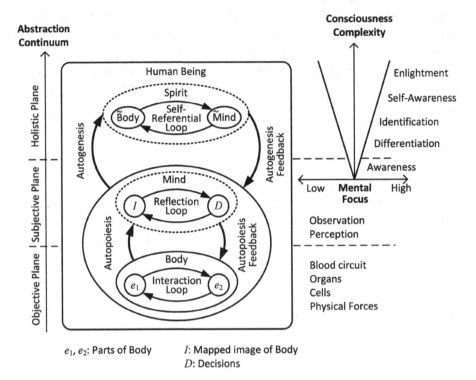

e_1, e_2: Parts of Body I: Mapped image of Body
D: Decisions

people perceive and understand their environment and deduce conclusions about it. Mental processes of conclusion and reflection lead to decisions that may then cause actions in the human's environment. Decisions may also cause reconsideration and adaption of internalized models.

Body and mind have a mutual influence on each other. This interaction is called "autopoiesis" denoting the emergence/immergence loop between the body (objective plane) and the mind (subjective plane).

Spirit

Human beings are spiritual beings. Body and mind are inseparable from each other and cannot be examined apart. From the first moment of formation of a human being, there is an autogenetic entanglement of these two aspects. At the holistic plane an existential essence arises, which we denote as a spiritual being. In this context, "spiritual" does not necessarily imply spirituality or believing in a higher power. It is understood here as a strong entanglement of body and mind with a consciousness as an epiphenomenon.

Consciousness

Consciousness is an epiphenomenon of the body-mind entanglement (cf. section "Consciousness Complexity" in chapter "URANOS: A Generic System Model"). The more intense this entanglement is, the higher stages of consciousness a human can reach. All stages of the consciousness complexity spectrum refer to a certain development of consciousness. Whenever a person reaches a certain stage of consciousness, this is a permanent acquisition (Wilber, 2007).

Example: Especially with children, the development of these stages clearly comes to light. P. Rochat identified several stages of self-awareness in the development of children. For a newborn, self-awareness is not fully available yet. Looking in a mirror the child does not recognize itself, but it experiences itself as someone else. With the development of the brain and the experiences gained in early life the child develops a sense of self and identification. These stages of consciousness are decisive for the later subsequent "me" of an adult (Rochat, 2003).

A human being can switch between different consciousness states. States characterize the mental focus of a human being and are of temporary nature (Gelernter, 1994). At high focus human thought is penetrating and analytical. As the focus is lowered thoughts are less penetrating and more relaxed. In general there are three major areas on that spectrum: awake (high-med focus), dreaming (low focus) and deep formless sleep (no focus) (Wilber, 2007).

Living Environment

Human beings are embedded in an environment. This allows human beings to interact with other entities, like objects, tools or other living or human beings. The environment is not only about physical reality, but includes all epistemological standpoints and their corresponding realities. Physical, informational and socio-cultural environments together form a *living environment* for human beings, who are connected to each of these environments through associated well-defined loops (Figure 2). This ensures that human beings are involved holistically, which is a prerequisite for stable and sustainable societies. It also underpins the fact that human beings enter into a symbiotic relationship with their living environment, so that they cannot be considered independent of their environment.

Figure 2. Interaction of a human being with its physical, informational and socio-cultural environments

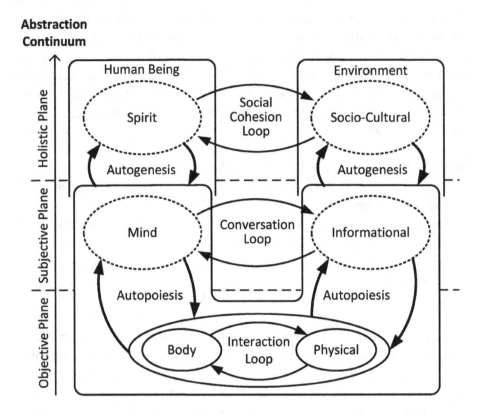

Physical Environment

The body is exposed to the physical environment. For instance radiation, chemicals and gravity influence the internal dynamics of the body. This environment contributes a significant portion of the well-being of a person.

Interactions in this environment are always dependent on space and time. If an interaction between two entities is taking place, then both entities must reside at a defined time and at a defined location.

Example: A man uses a shovel to dig a hole into the ground. At the time, when he wants to use the shovel, it must be locally available to him. He is not able to dig that hole if the shovel is too far away or not available before tomorrow. His physical interaction is space and time dependent.

Informational Environment

Human kind is one of the few species with comprehensively developed language skills. The term "language" is here understood in the general sense. In addition to spoken language, it also includes sign language and facial expressions. Language, together with communication and conversation processes, connects humans to an informational environment allowing them to share information with each other. This is a prerequisite for any mutual learning and beneficial collaboration. In this regard, observing, interpreting and imitating are very important patterns.

The informational environment allows humans to share their subjective reality very efficiently. In contrast to the physical environment and its associated interactions, the exchange through this environment can be independent of space and time.

Example: Modern technologies, such as the Internet and mobile computing, help people to share their ideas, thoughts and intentions. The shared information is embodied in text, pictures, sound or video messages. Communication platforms, like Facebook, iMessage or WhatsApp, allow to share information in an asynchronous manner, independently of location and time.

Socio-Cultural Environment

Social cohesion and culture emerge from interaction between human beings. Their existence appears beyond an individual mind, embracing the entire social group. Human beings are embedded in a socio-cultural environment, a space of humanity, welfare and culture. Because they are spiritual and social beings, missing or inadequate integration into this environment leads to great suffering and meaninglessness.

Interactions with the socio-cultural environment are also independent of space and time. The feeling of belonging to a social group will take place even if this group no longer physically exists.

Example: After World War II a Japanese soldier was found on Guam, a remote island in the Pacific Ocean. He did not notice (or ignored) that Japan capitulated in 1945. In the meantime, Japan went through a political and cultural change. When he returned in 1972, his social cohesion was still the same as that during the war (Gunkel, 2012). The social togetherness endured, even if the original social community changed or vanished in the meantime.

Human-to-Human Interaction

The proposed model for embedding humans into environments is also applicable for human-to-human interaction. In this context, the connecting loops express mutual influences on participating humans. It is important to notice that human-to-human interaction happens on all three levels. This means that all three loops are needed for collaborative behavior and long-term relations between humans.

Summary

In this instantiation of URANOS we presented a model for human beings. The dualistic mind-body problem is circumvented by considering human beings as a whole. Assuming that emergence/immergence loops exist, URANOS is instantiated for modeling human beings and their living environments.

The model considers human beings not only as bodies with mind, but also as spiritual beings. Body and mind are entangled, and a spirit emerges on the holistic plane. Consciousness is seen as an epiphenomenon emerging from this entanglement. Human beings are not completely independent and autonomous systems. They are social beings and need an environment in order to exist. Humans are embedded in an environment, which allows them to interact with each other. The environment consists of three subordinated levels to which humans are connected by loops: physical, informational and socio-cultural environments.

The model presented for human beings is also applicable for other living systems, like animals, be they mammals or reptiles. However, aspects like consciousness and spirituality might be different and would have to be adapted accordingly.

INTEGRAL THINKING

The goal of integral thinking is to include as many perspectives as possible into an interrelated network of approaches in order to deal with complex problems more successfully. Integral theory in this sense is a model based on a holistic standpoint (holism). It is a comprehensive consideration of many human disciplines in science, knowledge, humanities and arts. Therefore, it includes different perspectives, styles and methodologies in one model (Esbjörn, 2009).

In this section, the key concepts of integral theory are first explained. As a reference model we use the quadrant model, called *AQAL*, proposed by K. Wilber (1995). We show how AQAL is consistent with URANOS, focusing essentially on the similarities between the quadrants and the abstraction continuum. Finally, we present our integral dynamics of AQAL. We claim that this is an extension to the existing elements of AQAL allowing a deeper understanding of dynamics within and between perspectives.

The AQAL Model

The name AQAL stands for *all quadrants*, *all levels*, *all lines*, *all states*, and *all types*. It is a framework that allows holistic consideration of these five aspects for any complex system. The following text illustrates these aspects based on the work of K. Wilber (1995, 2007), S. Esbjörn-Hargens (2009), and V. Esbjörn-Hargens (2010).

All Quadrants

AQAL is based on at least four irreducible standpoints, which must be taken into account to understand any aspect of complex systems. Each of these standpoints, namely objective, subjective, interobjective and intersubjective, is placed on a quadrant. This leads to two fundamental distinctions: (1) the inside or outside of a system, and (2) the individual or collective view (Figure 3 - The placement of the quadrants was changed with respect to the original, so that they correlate with the abstraction continuum of URANOS).

The four quadrants also denote the four dimensions of reality. That is, each standpoint addresses a corresponding reality. Human beings have an individual internal state encompassing mind, spirit and consciousness. These entities are described by the individual-interior dimension (II), which refers to "I", the subjective standpoint of an individual. The physical body of a human is described by the individual-exterior dimension (IE), an objective standpoint referred to as "It". Humans as individuals are social beings, i.e. they form social groups. The collective-interior (CI) describes culture and world views, and represents the inter-subjective standpoint or "We". Finally, humans are embedded in physical and socio-cultural environments that are addressed by the collective-external dimension (CE), the "Its".

Figure 3. Each quadrant of the AQAL model describes a system from a specific perspective

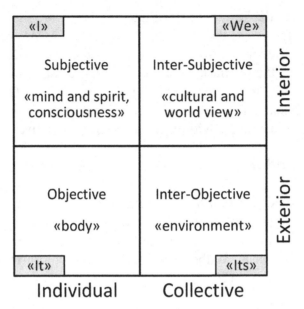

All Levels

Levels denote the long-term development of complex systems. They are present in all quadrants. In the case of exterior dimensions (IE and CE), ascending levels indicate increasing complexity of a system. On the other hand, in internal dimensions (II and CI) they describe the progressive depth, i.e. enfolding and entanglement of subjective aspects (Figure 4a).

Levels of each quadrant correlate to each other. This means reaching a certain level in a quadrant goes along with development within other quadrants. Together, levels form a *holarchy*, which is a kind of hierarchy where higher levels not only extend lower levels, but also include their essential aspects (Figure 4b).

Example: During the development from child to adult each consciousness level (II) goes along with the increasing complexity of the brain structure (IE). There is evidence that during adolescence, cognitive development is influenced by the neural maturation of the brain. This has an effect on the social and cultural behavior of young human beings (CI) as they become progressively self-aware and care about other people's opinions more intensively. In this period social relations to parents and friends start to change (CE) (Choudhury, Blakemore & Charman, 2006).

Figure 4. (a) Some levels of depth and complexity within the quadrants; (b) levels forming a holarchy

a)

b)

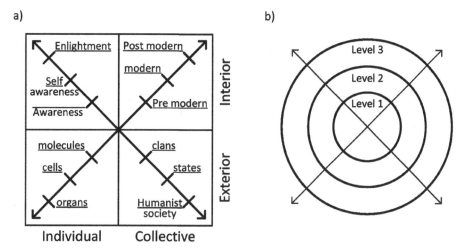

All Lines

Lines allow to illustrate the different developmental capacities of a system. They are just another way to indicate the different possibilities of development within the quadrants. For instance, there are several capacities a mind could develop, such as cognitive and emotional capacities:

Every complex system has its own development of these capacities. S. and V. Esbjörn-Hargens use the psychograph to illustrate the individual lines of development. It helps to identify the characteristics of a system. Similarly, the collective development capabilities are presented in a *sociograph*. Both can be drawn as charts, where the horizontal axis displays the lines of development and the vertical axis shows the levels of development (Figure 5) (S. Esbjörn-Hargens, 2009; V. Esbjörn-Hargens, 2010).

All States

The term "states" is used in AQAL to express temporary but distinct occurrences that alternately appear in the quadrants. They may be short-lived, temporary impressions and experience areas such as joy, sadness, fear or happiness in II. But greater state areas are also described, like waking, dreaming and deep dreamless sleep.

Different state groups may exist within each quadrant. Each group encompasses a set of states that are distinct from each other. For instance, a group of

Figure 5. Example of a pyschograph showing the levels of development for each line

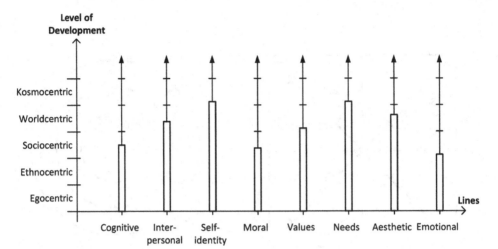

emotional states may include, among others, sadness and happiness. Within that group, an individual will only take one emotional state at a time, for it cannot be happy and sad at the same time.

States of different state groups are concurrent. The natural states of waking, dreaming and deep dreamless sleep may overlap with emotional states. For instance, while being asleep someone can feel sad.

All Types

The notion of types is used to classify things. Types are not clearly distinct from each other, but may overlap. They are used in all quadrants to describe the differences and characteristics of entities. For instance, in the individual-exterior quadrant, humans are divided into male and female. Or, in the collective-exterior quadrant, one could classify the different regime types, like democracy, autocracy or dictatorships.

Integral Abstraction Continuum

AQAL and URANOS are both universal and generic system models. AQAL is basically "entity-centered" describing entities from four perspectives, while URANOS is basically "interaction-centered", since the goal of URANOS is to estimate the dynamics between two or more entities. However, from an expressional power point of view, AQAL and URANOS are very convergent models.

In general, quadrants and levels can be mapped to URANOS. In the AQAL model, complexity increases towards the outside. URANOS describes complexity using the abstraction continuum, where complexity increases from bottom to top. In other words, levels do not originate from the center but from the bottom (Figure 6).

There are two fundamental differences between URANOS and AQAL, that should be mentioned: (1) scalability in the number of interacting systems considered (horizontal scalability); and (2) scalability in the number of perspectives (vertical scalability).

Horizontal Scalability

AQAL puts the system to study in the center of the four quadrants, examining it within the four perspectives. Studying two or more interacting systems requires separate AQAL instances accordingly. This leads to some redundancy, especially within their collective quadrants.

Figure 6. Quadrants and levels related to the abstraction continuum; the unity as additional areas above the quadrants describes explicitly holistic properties.

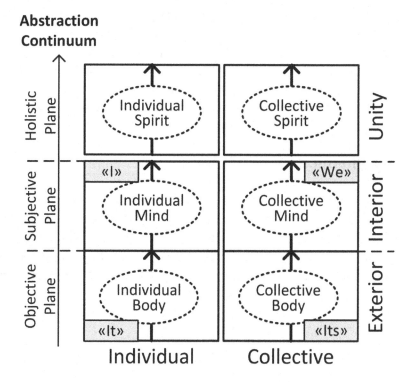

In URANOS, the individual and the collective aspects of an entity can be represented as two distinct entities. This approach allows to examine interactions between two or more entities, be it individual or collective entities. In this context, an individual entity is made of a body (IE) and a mind (II). A collective entity on the other hand may consist of different environments and other individuals. The physical environment (CE) describes external physical circumstances and groupings of entities. It is referred to as a *collective body*. The *collective mind* is formed by the common knowledge of individuals, and is embedded in an information environment (CI).

Vertical Scalability

URANOS describes enactive entities, be they individual or collective, in three planes, from objective, subjective and holistic standpoints. The holistic standpoint does not directly match to one of the quadrants in AQAL. This means that holistic and existential aspects cannot be described directly by a quadrant or any other notion in AQAL. Conversely, URANOS is basically considering an abstraction continuum that may be extended by other planes when necessary, describing novel and emerging aspects from new standpoints.

This holistic plane describes a *spirit*, which emerges through the entanglement of objective and subjective reality, i.e. exterior and interior. This spirit cannot be regarded as the exterior or interior of an entity, but is the *unity* of both. Therefore, two additional "quadrants" are added, one describing the unity of the individual entity, and the other one describing the collective entity. This scalability of perspectives even allows to describe aspects beyond holism, like aspects emerging from fourth-order systems (cf. section "Towards n-th order Systems" in chapter "URANOS: A Generic System Model").

System Dynamics

AQAL does not address system dynamics explicitly, while they are essential in URANOS. In that sense, URANOS can be used for extending the AQAL model with the new perspective of dynamics to explain how the four quadrants are maintained and influence each other. Additionally, it also addresses the dynamics from exterior and interior quadrants towards unity (Figure 7).

Figure 7. Dynamics within and between quadrants and towards the whole

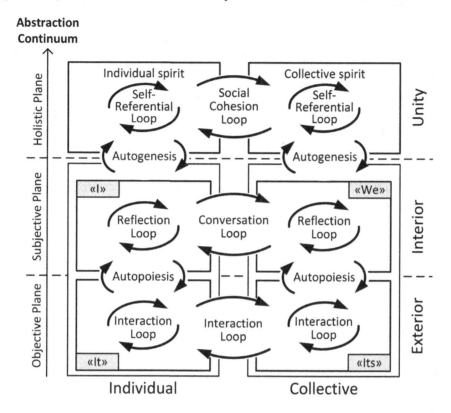

Exterior Dynamics

The dynamics of the exterior reality are described by interaction loops. Within both the IE and the CE quadrants, as well as between these two quadrants, interaction loops describe the transformation and the evolution from the objective standpoint.

Example: The human body is influenced by many circuits. Some are clearly within the body (IE), such as blood circulation and the nervous system. But a person breathes air and consumes food. These interactions happen between the human and its environment (CE). Finally, there are interactions outside the human body. They are indirectly coming into contact with humans, such as weather phenomena, or power generation in a power plant.

Interior Dynamics

The dynamics within the interior quadrants are designated by reflection loops. In the case of the individual-interior quadrant (II), reflection means decision-making and thinking about them. In II, mental processes determine the experiential phenomena of human beings. The cultural phenomena situated in the collective counterpart (CI) are maintained by cultural processes. Cultural change is accompanied by feedback, enabling a collective reflection and finally challenging transformations.

The interior of individuals is coupled with the collective counterpart. In this sense, individuals are part of the collective and make their contributions. Their actions must always be considered in the context of the collective. With the feedback of the collective, the individual learns the applicable socio-cultural rules and can adapt his actions. This is one of the basic prerequisites so that individuals can join together in social groups, developing a common understanding of values and goals. These dynamics between individual-interior and collective-interior are described by the conversation loop.

Exterior-Interior Dynamics

Between the exterior and interior there are dynamics that describe their mutual effects. The internalization of the exterior, and its feedback, are described by the autopoietic loop.

There is a close relation between behavior (IE) and experiential phenomena (II) of human beings. Human behavior is the embodiment of his mental and psychological states, which are hidden in the human mind. Conversely, the knowledge and experience of a person comes in large part from their activity, like learning-by-doing. This also holds for the collective counterpart. For instance, damages caused to the environment (CE) are often the result of cultural phenomena (CI). And conversely, changes in the environment can also lead to cultural changes.

Dynamics towards the Unity

The dynamics of the exterior-interior entanglement are described by the self-referential loop. It describes the inseparable interaction between these two realities and is the cause for higher consciousness and spirituality. This applies equally to an individual and a collective.

The dynamics between individual and collective spirits are described by the social cohesion loop. It expresses the socio-cultural affiliation and cohesion of the individual towards the collective. That is, the individual and the collective merge into one wholeness.

Summary

Integral thinking means including as many perspectives as possible in order to obtain a comprehensive and holistic picture of a system. The AQAL model is one of several ways to structure and interrelate the different perspectives and realities of complex systems. AQAL defines five aspects that enable a holistic approach, including all quadrants, all levels, all lines, all states and all types. Based on this model an instantiation of URANOS has been presented.

From an expressional power point of view, AQAL and URANOS are very convergent models. Nevertheless, they differ in the way they describe systems. AQAL is "entity-centered" describing an entity from four perspectives, whereas URANOS is "interaction-centered" focusing on the dynamics between entities. We showed how the quadrants of AQAL can be mapped to the abstraction continuum of URANOS. In this context, a fundamental difference is mentioned, namely that URANOS can be extended by new perspectives, whereas AQAL is limited to the four perspectives. Thus, emerging characteristics and dynamics can be described in URANOS explicitly.

As a new finding URANOS extends AQAL with a sixth aspect, *dynamics*. Dynamics govern complex systems, especially within and between the different realities (quadrants). This aspect allows a deeper understanding on how complex systems behave, and how realities and their entities influence each others.

COORDINATION MODEL

Coordination is an integral aspect of complex and dynamic systems. In this section, we want to limit ourselves to the following two areas: multi-agent systems (MASs) and cyber-physical systems (CPSs). MASs serve as a reference model for helping to understand distributed concurrent processes. Cyber-physical systems are a concrete modeling approach, where computing processes are embedded in the physical world.

The goal of this section is to present a coordination model which is based on URANOS and applicable for technical systems. This section starts with an introduction to coordination in the context of computer science, in particular through the examples of MASs and CPSs. Then, a coordination model is presented. It is based on a spectrum illustrating coordination from the objective, subjective and holistic standpoints.

Coordination for Computer Science

Coordination is a generic concept designating the management of interactions and dependencies between entities. Therefore, it has significant influence on the evolution of a system. In terms of our generic system model, we define coordination as:

Definition [Coordination]: Coordination is the management of evolution, that is controlling and directing interactions.

Coordination has been extensively studied in the field of computer science and artificial intelligence, e.g. Gelernter & Carriero (1992), Hirsbrunner et al. (1994), Maffioletti et al. (2004). We intend to give a glimpse of how coordination is understood in relation to two research objects: multi-agent systems (MASs) and cyber-physical systems (CPSs).

Multi-Agent Systems

Multi-agent systems (MASs) are computerized and distributed systems based on interacting agents (Ferber, 1999; Woolridge & Wooldridge, 2001). An agent is a computer system that is able to act independently and autonomously in relation to the system's user. In a multi agent system the agents have to cooperate, coordinate and negotiate with each other in order to successfully perform their work. Among others, MASs deal with key problems like how agents can be built that carry out their work independently and autonomously; and how agents can coordinate their work and cooperate with other agents.

On the one hand, MASs serve to solve complex problems that are difficult or impossible to solve by single agent systems, i.e. monolithic systems. MASs have been successfully implemented in real applications, such as in meteorology, space exploration or in computer games. On the other hand, the concept of a MAS is used to study the distributed and concurrent acting of agents within a shared environment. In this context, there are several aspects of interest including self-organization, distributed learning, social behaviors and notably coordination and collaboration between agents. This study is also referred to as *agent-based modeling (ABM)* (Macal & North, 2010).

Coordination has been extensively studied with respect to MASs. In a proposal by M. Schumacher, coordination is divided into objective and subjective aspects (Schumacher, 2001). Objective coordination mainly describes the organization and the interaction of agents from an objective standpoint. Subjective coordination treats the dependencies between agents that arise within the mind of an agent. In this context, important aspects are perception, mental processes and decisions-making.

A more comprehensive and integral approach in this direction is MASQ (Multi-Agent Systems based on Quadrants) (Ferber, Stratulat & Tranier, 2009). MASQ is inspired by integral thinking, in particular by the AQAL-model of K. Wilber (2007). In this sense, the design and analysis of a MAS is performed on the two dimensions: the individual-collective dimension and the exterior-interior dimension. Ferber et al. mentioned four principles or assumptions for MASQ: (1) body and mind are separate but connected entities; (2) the mind is an entity of integrity and cannot be directly accessed from outside; (3) an actor can only influence the dynamics of the environment, and cannot directly control it; (4) an agent may have besides a physical also a social body, which expresses its roles in social groups; and (5) the distinction of the physical (brute) environment and the socio-cultural environment. Their approach aims to bring MAS closer to real world situations.

Cyber-Physical Systems

Cyber-physical systems (CPSs) aim to bring computing power to the physical reality. A big challenge is to integrate the world of physical and engineered systems with the domain of computing and logic. There are various approaches to designing such systems. Some are very similar to MASs. In CPSs, computational units (like agents and services) are often, but not exclusively, embedded in the physical environment. They perceive the physical circumstances and act accordingly. Other concepts of CPSs propose that only sensors and actuators are placed in the physical environment. The actual computing and control system is located somewhere on the Internet (Simmon et al., 2013) (ex. Cloud computing, Internet of Things).

CPSs often have to cope with a very heterogeneous world. Various devices and protocols are combined to form a whole. For instance, service-oriented coordination helps to purposefully process information in a network of services (Maffioletti, Kouadri & Hirsbrunner, 2004). Each physical device provides their own semantic purpose when being integrated into the system. This allows to handle it more adaptively.

A complicating factor is that these systems are designed to work with people, not only logically but also physically. It means that the system aims to support humans in their activities and should identify critical situations (Bruegger, 2011). This is often referred to as *human-in-the-loop*. It is a concept focusing on how humans are integrated into CPSs, especially as part of control loops. The latest research on CPSs tends to integrate the socio-cultural aspects of humans with the cyber and physical dimensions. Examples are the anthropocentric CPS (Zamfirescu, Pirvu, Loskyll & Zuehlke, 2014), the socio-cyber-physical systems (Frazzon, Hartmann, Makuschewitz & Scholz-Reiter, 2013), or the NSF's cyber-human systems program (National Science Foundation, 2016).

Our Approach

Our instantiation is based on the principle of objective-subjective coordination. But, from our standpoint, it is also important to take into account the cognitive and holistic aspects of human beings. Therefore, the coordination model must include, beside objective and subjective aspects, the cognitive and emotional capabilities of the human beings.

We propose an agent model that corresponds to the perceptual control loop of URANOS (Figure 8). Intelligent agents are autonomous entities that pursue a goal that can be given by other agents or humans. Through sensors, agents perceive their surroundings causing a subjective image of the current situation. In this sense, images, acquired knowledge, goals and intentions lead to decisions. They express how the agent will respond to that current situation. Finally, changes in the environment are caused by actuators.

Henceforth, we use the term "smart entity" for intelligent agents, and "enactive entities" for human-like agents.

Coordination Spectrum

If complex systems encompass interacting smart and enactive entities, then dependencies between entities arise on all three abstraction planes. Accordingly, the dependencies are divided into objective, subjective and cognitive dependencies (Schumacher, 2001; Hadorn, Courant & Hirsbrunner, 2014a). They have to be managed by appropriate coordination processes on each plane. This leads to different coordination concepts, which are named objective, subjective and cognitive coordination.

Figure 8. An agent model based on perceptual control theory (Powers et al., 2008).

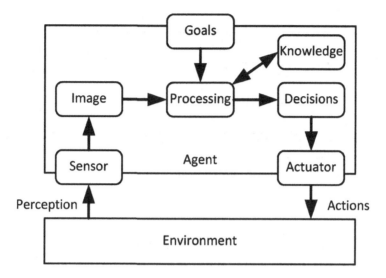

Often, there is no sharp differentiation between these concepts. Therefore, we propose a *coordination spectrum*, which correlates with the abstraction continuum of URANOS (Figure 9).

Objective Coordination

Interacting entities are the subject for objective coordination (Figure 10). They are named *coordinatables*. Typically, they are located in a space where the coordination takes place, called the *coordination media* C_M. It denotes the boundary within which coordinatables are managed and organized. Inside this media certain rules govern the behavior of coordinatables. The sum of all rules is referred to as *coordination law* C_L.

Figure 9. Coordination spectrum, which describes the management of dependencies from the standpoint of objectivism, subjectivism and holism

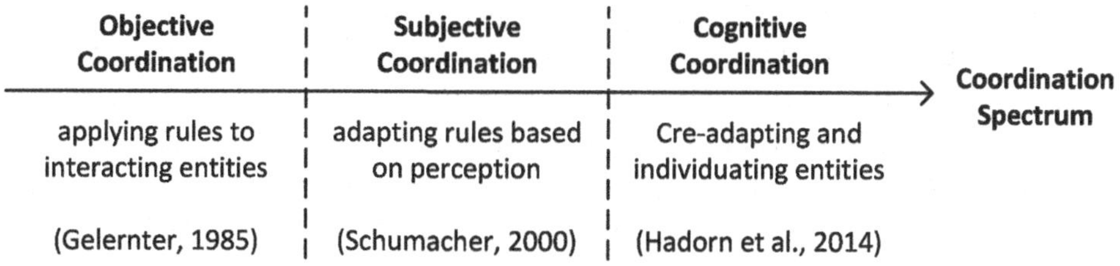

Objective Coordination	Subjective Coordination	Cognitive Coordination	
applying rules to interacting entities	adapting rules based on perception	Cre-adapting and individuating entities	Coordination Spectrum
(Gelernter, 1985)	(Schumacher, 2000)	(Hadorn et al., 2014)	

Figure 10. Objective coordination model describing the application of rules to interacting entities

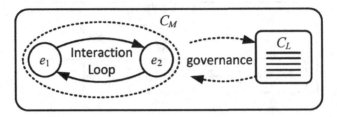

e_1,e_2: Coordinatables
C_L: Coordination Law (Rules)
C_M: Coordination Media

Objective coordination processes manage the evolution of the system. They concern two things: (1) organization of the media, and (2) triggering rules to manage the interactions between entities (Schumacher, 2000). The organization describes the structural aspects of a system, i.e. how entities are arranged within the media. Different forms of organization can be realized, such as hierarchies and networks. The management of interactions deals with system dynamics. In this sense, coordination processes describe how entities interact, communicate and work together by offering suitable infrastructure.

Coordination does not necessarily need a centralized or specialized entity, like a coordinator. For instance, in self-organization, coordination happens spontaneously by applying rules implicitly to coordinatables.

Subjective Coordination

Subjectivity arises when smart entities perceive their surroundings and start building their own relationships with their surroundings. The process of building these relationships is individual and prevents the assumption that there is a "common reality" behind the entities' experience, rather it is a subjective reality. In this context, smart entities develop subjective dependencies on other entities. The management of these dependencies is referred to as *subjective coordination* (Schumacher, 2000).

To one extent, subjective coordination processes manage *mental processes*, that are perceiving, processing, making decisions and finally adapting the coordination law (Omicini & Ossowski, 2003a). This management is fundamental, especially for goal-driven smart entities. They act more or less autonomously within a coordination media. Through autopoiesis, they distinguish themselves from the media, and through perception they are capable of internalizing external states of that media. Together with previously acquired knowledge, intentions and goals, smart entities make decisions about how they have to act in order to pursue their goals (Figure 11).

To another extent, subjective coordination also deals with *inter-entity conversation*. Whereas objective coordination processes provide infrastructure for communication, subjective coordination processes guide the conversation itself. This allows smart entities to exchange information, to negotiate and get a mutual agreement of their common goals. Conversation is a requirement, so that participating entities can agree on their goals and actions, and notably can coordinate their activities in a mutually beneficial manner (Dubberly & Pangaro, 2009).

Cognitive Coordination

When dealing with enactive entities (e.g. human beings or other living systems), holistic coordination processes involving shared knowledge, creativity and empathy become relevant to the system. We use the term *cognitive coordination* to refer to these new emerging aspects (Figure 12).

Figure 11. Subjective coordination model extending the objective coordination model with the management of subjective dependencies

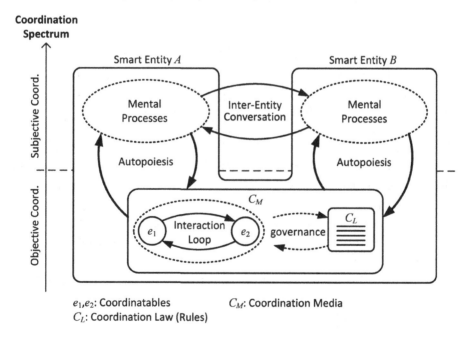

e_1, e_2: Coordinatables C_M: Coordination Media
C_L: Coordination Law (Rules)

Figure 12. Cognitive coordination model dealing with dependencies arising on the holistic plane such as creativity and empathy

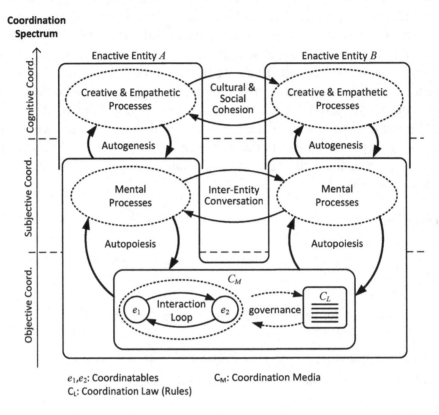

The way an enactive entity finds new strategies to achieve its goals may have great influence on the overall system development. Cognitive coordination processes help to manage and support inspiration and creativity; and ethics, beliefs and emotions accompany these processes.

Cognitive coordination processes also manage the dependencies that arise within social groups, such as social and cultural cohesion. For instance, they manage the way human beings must be integrated in social and cultural environments, so that they feel themselves as a part of them (e.g. immigration and integration programs).

Cognitive coordination may also reinforce enthusiasm. As G. Hüther states (2012), enthusiasm is a major reason for high performance learning, because it causes the brain to reconfigure and create new structures. In this sense, cognitive coordination processes encourage and inspire human beings to develop innovative and creative findings. It is far more than brain storming processes, but allows self-fulfillment of human beings. And that leads to enthusiasm.

Summary

The instantiation of URANOS towards a coordination model fills the gap between holistic and cognitive coordination processes. The proposed model is based on a coordination spectrum. Objective coordination processes manage inter-entity dependencies, like organization of the environment, as well as interactions between entities. Subjective coordination processes deal with the intra-entity dependencies that arise with perceptual capabilities of smart entities. Appropriate processes manage these dependencies within the mind of an entity, and the exchanges between entities through conversation. Finally, cognitive coordination handles holistic dependencies that emerge with the integration of enactive entities, like human beings.

CONCLUSION

We identified three core models that are important for human-centered design. Each one has been introduced as an instantiation of URANOS, namely the body-mind continuum, AQAL and coordination. We then showed that URANOS is able to describe and sometimes extend these three models.

The body-mind continuum describes humans as holistic and spiritual beings. For human-centered systems (HCSs) this model contributes to a holistic and comprehensive consideration of human beings within complex, technical and social systems. An important statement is that humans, although autonomous, are also fundamentally involved in interaction with their environment, which hence forth strongly influences them through conversation loops. In this context, the environment is not purely physical, it also encompasses informational and socio-cultural aspects.

The AQAL-model as part of integral thinking provides a holistic view onto complex systems. It combines different perspectives into one model, such as objectivity and subjectivity. AQAL is extended by the perspective of explicit dynamics, which allows deeper understanding of system dynamics and development. Along with the body-mind continuum, this enables holistic and comprehensive modeling of human beings and technical systems alike. In addition, it facilitates the derivation of some principles for human-centered design, like participation, equity and responsiveness. These are described in more detail within the next chapter.

The coordination model concerns managing interactions between entities within a complex system. It is a cornerstone for designing goal-directed systems. Coordination describes processes leading to self-organization and collaboration between entities, so that the entire system fulfills its purpose. In this sense, coordination happens on all levels of abstraction. A new concept we have brought is cognitive coordination. It enables the description of processes managing inspiration, creativity and empathy among enactive entities.

With URANOS as a common denominator, it is possible to combine these three models together into one model for human-centered design. This is a big advantage compared to other approaches, because humans and technology can now be treated as entities on equal footing, each in its manifestation as an enactive and smart entity respectively. Dynamics and processes connect people with technology in a way that enables purposeful and profitable collaboration between them.

REFERENCES

Bruegger, P. (2011). *uMove: a wholistic framework to design and implement ubiquitous computing systems supporting user's activity and situation* (Doctoral dissertation). Retrieved from réro Doc. (R006095784)

Choudhury, S., Blakemore, S. J., & Charman, T. (2006). Social cognitive development during adolescence. *Social Cognitive and Affective Neuroscience*, *1*(3), 165–174. doi:10.1093/scan/nsl024 PMID:18985103

Davids, T. W. R., Stede, W. & Pâli Text Society. (1921). *The Pali Text Society's Pali-English Dictionary*. London, UK: The Pali Text Society.

Descartes, R. (1968). Discourse on Method and the Meditations (F. Sutcliffe, Trans.). New York, NY: Penguin Books Limited. (Originally published 1637 and 1641)

Dubberly, H., & Pangaro, P. (2009). On Modeling - What is conversation, and how can we design for it? *Interaction*, *16*(4), 22–28. doi:10.1145/1551986.1551991

Esbjörn-Hargens, S. (2009, March). *An Overview of Integral Theory: An All-Inclusive Framework for the 21st Century* (Resource Paper No. 1). Louisville, CO: Integral Institute.

Esbjörn-Hargens, V. (2010). Psychograph as map, matrix, and mirror: An integral psychograph assessment. *Journal of Integral Theory & Practice*, *5*, 21–58.

Ferber, J. (1999). *Multi-Agent Systems: An Introduction to Distributed Artificial Intelligence*. Boston, MA: Addison-Wesley Longman Publishing Co., Inc.

Ferber, J., Stratulat, T., & Tranier, J. (2009). Towards an Integral Approach of Organizations in Multi-Agent Systems. In V. Dignum (Ed.), *Handbook of Research on Multi-Agent Systems: Semantics and Dynamics of Organizational Models*. Hershey, PA: Information Science Reference. doi:10.4018/978-1-60566-256-5.ch003

Frazzon, E. M., Hartmann, J., Makuschewitz, T. & Scholz-Reiter, B. (2013). Towards Socio-Cyber-Physical Systems in Production Networks. *Procedia {CIRP}*, *7*, 49-54.

Gelernter, D. H. (1994). *The Muse in the Machine: Computerizing the Poetry of Human Thought*. New York, NY: The Free Press.

Gelernter, D. H., & Carriero, N. (1992). Coordination Languages and their Significance. *Communications of the ACM*, *35*(2), 97–107. doi:10.1145/129630.129635

Gunkel, C. (2012). *Der einsame Kampf des Soldaten Yokoi*. Retrieved from http://www.spiegel.de/einestages/spaetes-weltkriegsende-a-947462.html

Hadorn, B., Courant, M., & Hirsbrunner, B. (2014a). *A Holistic Approach to Cognitive Coordination*. Fribourg, Switzerland: University of Fribourg.

Hirsbrunner, B., Aguilar, M., & Krone, O. (1994a). CoLa: A Coordination Language for Massive Parallelism. In *Proceedings ACM Symposium on Principles of Distributed Computing (PODC)*. New York, NY: ACM. doi:10.1145/197917.198156

Hüther, G. (2012). Learning enthusiastically. A conversation with Prof. Dr. Gerald Hüther. *Televizion*, *25*, 14–15.

Macal, C. M., & North, M. J. (2010). Tutorial on Agent-based Modelling and Simulation. *Journal of Simulation*, *4*(3), 151–162. doi:10.1057/jos.2010.3

Maffioletti, S. (2006). *UbiDev: A Homogeneous Service Framework for Pervasive Computing Environments* (Doctoral dissertation). Retrieved from réro Doc. (R004526374)

Maffioletti, S., Kouadri, M. S., & Hirsbrunner, B. (2004). A Holistic Approach for Pervasive Computing Environments.*Communication Networks and Distributed Systems Modeling and Simulation Conference, 2004*. San Diego, CA: CNDS.

National Science Foundation. (2016, July). *Cyber-Human Systems (CHS)*. Retrieved from http://www.nsf.gov/cise/iis/chs_pgm13.jsp

Omicini, A., & Ossowski, S. (2003a). Objective versus Subjective Coordination in the Engineering of Agent Systems. In M. Klusch, S. Bergamaschi, P. Edwards, & P. Petta (Eds.), *Intelligent Information Agents* (Vol. 2586, pp. 179–202). Berlin, Germany: Springer. doi:10.1007/3-540-36561-3_9

Poteat, W. H. (1985). Polanyian Meditations. In *Search of a Post-Critical Logic*. Durham, NC: Duke University Press.

Powers, W. T., Abbott, B., Carey, T. A., Goldstein, D. M., Mansell, W., Marken, R. S., & Taylor, M. et al. (2008). Perceptual Control Theory - A Model for Understanding the Mechanisms and Phenomena of Control. In D. Forssell (Ed.), *Perceptual Control Theory: Science & Applications: A Book of Readings* (pp. 18–34). Living Control Systems Publishing.

Rochat, P. (2003). Five levels of self-awareness as they unfold early in life. *Consciousness and Cognition*, *12*(4), 717–731. doi:10.1016/S1053-8100(03)00081-3 PMID:14656513

Schumacher, M. (2000). *Designing and Implementing Objective Coordination in Multi-Agent Systems*. Retrieved from PAI-Research Group, University of Fribourg: https://diuf.unifr.ch/main/pai/node/205

Schumacher, M. (2001). *Objective Coordination in Multi-Agent System Engineering: Design and Implementation*. Berlin, Germany: Springer-Verlag. doi:10.1007/3-540-44933-7

Schwarz, E., & Dubois, D. M. (2010). On the Nature of Consciousness - On Consciousness in Nature. *AIP Conference Proceedings*, *1303*, 334–342. doi:10.1063/1.3527171

Simmon, E., Kim, K. S., Subrahmanian, E., Lee, R., De Vaulx, F., Murakami, Y., & Sriram, R. D. et al. (2013). *A Vision of Cyber-physical Cloud Computing for Smart Networked Systems. National Institute of Standards and Technology*. NIST. doi:10.6028/NIST.IR.7951

Wilber, K. (1995). *Sex, Ecology, Spirituality: The Spirit of Evolution*. Boston, MA: Shambhala Publications.

Wilber, K. (2007). *The Integral Vision: A Very Short Introduction to the Revolutionary Integral Approach to Life, God, the Universe, and Everything*. Boston, MA: Shambhala Publications.

Woolridge, M., & Wooldridge, M. J. (2001). *Introduction to Multiagent Systems*. New York, NY: John Wiley & Sons, Inc.

Zamfirescu, C. B., Pirvu, B. C., Loskyll, M., & Zuehlke, D. (2014). Do Not Cancel My Race with Cyber-Physical Systems. *Proceedings of the 19th World Congress of the International Federation of Automatic Control*. Laxenburg, Austria: IFAC. doi:10.3182/20140824-6-ZA-1003.01600

ENDNOTE

[1]   We would rather prefer the term "body-mind problem", since our continuum expands from body towards mind and spirit.

Chapter 4
Towards Human–Centered System Design

ABSTRACT

Based on URANOS and its instantiations for human beings, integral thinking and coordination, this chapter presents a model for human-machine collaboration. Nine design principles are presented. They ensure that designing and operating human-centered systems respects human integrity in any human-machine collaboration, i.e. not harmed, or enslaved, reduced, etc. A central component of this model is the conversation between human and machine. It allows humans and machines to enter into an adaptive learning organization, a prerequisite for any mutual beneficial collaboration. Finally, a concrete use case addressing smart industrial machines operating in the context of the fourth industrial revolution is presented.

INTRODUCTION

Human-centered systems (HCSs) put human beings in the center of their design and working processes (Gill, Funston, Thrope, Hijitaka & Gotze, 1993). In this chapter, we show how URANOS can be applied for HCSs, as a complex technical system encompassing human beings and their socio-cultural environment. In this context of designing human-centered systems, the three instantiations presented in chapter "Model Instantiations", namely body-mind continuum, coordination model and integral thinking, are put together into one model for human-machine collaboration.

DOI: 10.4018/978-1-5225-1888-4.ch004

Several design principles are needed to ensure that such systems respect human integrity. Special attention is paid to compliance with human values, in particular preserving of human integrity in any human-machine symbiosis, i.e. not harmed, or slaved, reduced, etc. Based on these principles a design is presented showing how smart machines may converse and collaborate with human beings. In this sense, humans and machines are holistically integrated into a system, allowing them to achieve their common goals through collaboration.

First, in section "Human-Centered Systems: State of the Art" an introduction to HCSs is given, presenting the state of the art of HCSs, and showing how the three instantiations of URANOS are related to HCSs. Section "Design Principles" presents the major design principles that form the base of human-centered design. Section "Model for Human-Machine Collaboration" explains a model for human-machine symbiosis that goes beyond classical human-machine interaction. A concrete design based on that model is presented in section "Designing Smart Industrial Machines: A Case Study". Some conclusions are given in section "Conclusion".

HUMAN-CENTERED SYSTEMS: STATE OF THE ART

Designing an HCS is about putting humans in the center of design and system processes (Gill et al., 1993). The term "human-centered" is often mistaken for "user-centered". User-centered design regards humans as technology users. In contrast to that, human-centered design opens the scope to also include the social and organizational context of users, system designers, engineers, and other persons affected by the system (Gasson, 2003).

This section gives an overview of three important aspects of HCSs. First, an outline of the background and related work of HCS is given. Then, Schwartz's theory of universal human values is presented in the context of HCSs. Then, human-centered design is brought to light in relation to positive emotions, such as enthusiasm. And finally, some background on bio-cost and stress as quantitative metrics is presented.

Human-Centered Approaches

Human-centered approaches began to evolve in the 1990's. They emerged from the vision of letting human beings participate in the system processes while taking into account their social and cultural contexts. K.S. Gill (1996) argued, that "human-centredness expounds an emancipatory tradition which places human needs, purpose, skill, creativity, and human potential at the centre of activities of human organisations and the design of technical systems" (p. 1). He stated that the idea of human-machine symbiosis is central in approaching human-centered design, as there will be a symbiotic relationship between humans and machines. According to M. Cooley (2008), in the context of HCS, the human handles the qualitative and subjective aspects, and the machine manages the quantitative elements of that relation. The symbiosis may encompass not only a single machine and a single human being, but could include a network of machines and human beings (Gill, 1996).

Human-centered computing (HCC) is a research discipline which deals with computer technologies and human beings, and the way they interact with each other. HCC has its roots in, among others, human-computer interaction (HCI), user-centered design and computer-supported cooperative work (CSCW). As mentioned by A. Jaimes et al. (2007), "HCC facilitates the design of effective computer systems that take into account personal, social, and cultural aspects and addresses issues such as information design, human-information interaction, human-computer interaction, human-human interaction, and the relationships between computing technology and art, social, and cultural issues" (p. 31). They mentioned three main characteristics of HCC: (1) the system must encounter human abilities and limitations on an individual basis; (2) it must be aware of socio-cultural issues; and (3) it must be adaptive in terms of interacting with individuals and in special situations.

Human Values

Existential and social values are important to human beings. S.H. Schwartz (2006) presents a value theory based on fundamental human values, which are motivationally distinguished from each other. They are derived from the "needs of individuals as biological organisms, requisites of coordinated social interaction, and survival and welfare needs of groups" (p. 2). Values correspond to beliefs that characterize abstract goals. They enable humans to select or guide their activities as they serve as standards (Schwartz, 2006).

As proposed by S.H. Schwartz, values are culturally universal. This can be explained by the evolutionary development of humans. When experiencing a situation, certain regions in the brain are triggered to guide the activities and behavior of the human being. There is also a region for basic moral behavior, which causes people to stand up for human values, no matter what culture they belong to. Of course, there are differences in the way each brain reacts, and from a social perspective there may exist misconducts. The different values are ordered by their individual and subjective importance in the brain.

Due to culture, education and experiences these priorities may change, leading to an individualized and personal hierarchy of value importance. In this sense, values and their priorities are not static, but underly the evolutionary development of human beings and their societies.

In Schwartz's value theory, human values are grouped in two orthogonal dimensions: (1) openness vs. conservation, and (2) self-enhancement vs. self-transcendence (Figure 1). And there is one special value, hedonism, that belongs to both dimensions.

Openness vs. Conservation

The first dimension describes the values in the tension between openness and conservation. Openness includes self-determination in thought and action, freedom of choice, and creativity. It also comprises stimulation to discover and explore new aspects of life. These values are antagonist to conservative values focusing on social security, conformity, and maintaining traditions.

Figure 1. Theoretical model of human values, showing the two dimensions of openness to conservation and self-enhancement to self-transcendence (Schwartz, 2006).

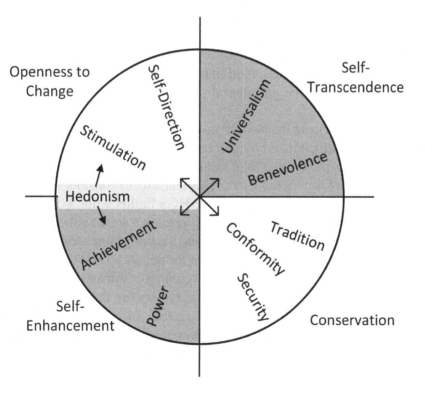

Self-Enhancement vs. Self-Transcendence

The opposed values of self-enhancement and self-transcendence form a second dimension. Self-enhancement comprises values for the recognition of personal achievements and the claim to power. On the other hand, there are values of self-transcendence, such as helpfulness, benevolence, social justice and equality (universalism).

Hedonism

Pleasure and joy intrinsically enhance people's lives and make them more valuable. In contrast, frustrations, suffering and pain complicate their lives. This principle is referred to as *prudential hedonism* (Weijers, 2016).

Hedonism as a value is associated to both openness and self-enhancement. Positive emotions, such as pleasure and enthusiasm, promote the ability of people to discover and learn new things. And, it also increases the feeling of self-worth.

Integral Design

Design is a process of intentional creation or arrangement of processes and components, so that the resulting system fulfills a desired purpose. Often, this process is not carried out by the same people who are supposed to operate the system. Nor can it be assumed that design and operation are sequential processes. Design can be an integral process throughout the lifecycle of a system.

People who carry out the design process are called *designers*. The system that is created or customized by the design process, bears an impression of the designer. This means that their thoughts, spirits and enthusiasm hover in the system and are felt by the users. This leads us to consider that designers belong to the system as users do. Thus, HCS builds a link between people from the first moment of its existence. It creates a social cohesion.

Good design mediates the relevance and meaningfulness of a system. This is one of the most important prerequisites for people so that they can develop positive emotions about a system. Brain research confirms that positive emotions, like enthusiasm and pleasure, strongly improve the skills and learning abilities of human beings (Hüther, 2012, 2016). In contrast, bad design can cause negative emotions such as frustration, anger and suffering. Moreover, this has a negative impact on the use of the system. And due to social cohesion, it also transmits frustration to others within a social environment. This negative spiral has a fatal effect on people, like stress, burn-out and futility of human life, and on societies, like rebellion and extremism.

Design decisions often have much greater impact than that of which designers are aware. Therefore, it is important that designers and users see themselves as part of the whole system, surrounded by dynamics that connect them.

Bio-Costs

An important goal of human-centered design is the reduction of human bio-costs. A bio-cost is defined as a "measurable, biological cost to any system performing an activity in pursuit of 'getting what it wants'" (Geoghegan & Pangaro, 2008). It covers the key resources of time, attention and energy that a living system has to expend for its activities. Bio-cost also includes the emotional factor of stress which occurs due to the shared and limited nature of these resources. Bio-costs are quantitative metrics in system design, which have to be minimized.

Our Approach

An HCS must be devoted to human values and welfare. Ignoring some values would lead to simplification or reduction of the human being. And that could give rise to negative emotions and to the rejection of that system. Similarly, high bio-costs and stress may lead to the abandonment of the system too. Devotion to human values and reduction of bio-cost are therefore integral parts of any human-centered design. Designers and users must always keep this in mind.

From our generic standpoint, an HCS must consider the following basic aspects: (1) it must holistically integrate humans as enactive entities - this includes the different levels of interaction, conversation and social cohesion. (2) It must be devoted to human values and help to reduce the bio-costs of humans. And (3), it must adapt to the evolution of humans and their social communities enabling new human activities to arise. Building such systems implies having a model that handles all relevant entities consistently (e.g. humans and machines) (Hadorn, Courant & Hirsbrunner, 2015b, 2016b).

We propose a model for human-machine collaboration, which is based on the body-mind continuum, integral thinking and cognitive coordination. This model is guided by design principles for human-centered design.

DESIGN PRINCIPLES

Human-centered design ensures that an HCS is acceptable for human-beings and their environment. The aim of this section is to highlight and explain its major design principles[1]. Generally, they are used to perceive people as holistic beings and to consider them as such during the lifecycle of an HCS. These principles form the basis of human-centered design in our sense. The goal of these design principles is to guide the design process, preventing frustration and empowering enthusiasm.

It is not an exhaustive list, and new principles may be added as this research continues. Our feeling is that these principles are sufficient for a first prototype.

Devotion to Human Values

Putting human beings in the center of design processes implies a devotion to human values. The goal of this principle is to preserve human dignity and integrity in any human-machine symbiosis.

Formally, an HCS must comply with the local legal framework and must fully protect human rights. Systems violating humanity, existential or social values cannot be regarded as human-centered.

Also, weaker values, such as hedonism, self-direction, security, power and benevolence, must be adequately accommodated in the design. It is important to note that the priorities of human values differ from one person to another. The design should respond dynamically and situationally to changed value priorities.

Equity/Inclusiveness

Often, only users are considered when designing systems. We propose to break through this narrow definition and to enlarge the circle. Every person who comes into contact with an HCS during its lifecycle, should be part of the design, e.g. designer, stake holders and users, and even the maid.

The integration of humans into an HCS is a critical task. Humans should be considered in the design of HCS as holistic beings. Looking at URANOS, there is a circuit on each abstraction plane connecting them with other entities (e.g. systems, other humans). The design of an HCS should explicitly address these circuits, making them comfortable and suitable for human beings.

HCSs should ensure that human beings are not discriminated against: that people are not excluded nor reduced according to their origin, race, culture, age and sex.

Example: If a system is used by people with disabilities, then their disability should be taken into account accordingly. For example, public transport as an HCS should provide ticketing machines which are easily operable by blind people. Similarly, for elderly people, whose movements may be less accurate, font and button sizes must be adapted accordingly.

Adaptivity

Human beings and their environments are constantly changing. HCSs must adapt to the evolution of humans and their social communities supporting new emerging human activities. The principle of adaptivity takes this into account.

Static design and implementations are indeed easier to realize. However, the resulting systems often prevent quick response to changing needs and circumstances. They have to be redesigned manually, which is an expensive and time consuming task. And, in the worst case, such systems no longer meet the new requirements. Their behavior is perceived as disturbing.

The principle of adaptivity includes the following two key points: (1) the design process never ends as long as a system is used by human beings; and (2) human needs, skills and creativity are considered constantly in the design process. This allows people to self-realize when working with an HCS.

Responsiveness

In HCSs, responsiveness refers to two things: (1) requests of human beings need to be handled in a reasonable time frame; and (2) the way human beings exchange and acquire knowledge in HCSs.

The principle of responsiveness addresses a reactive human-machine interface. Here, human beings expect feedback within an expected time frame when they interact with the machine. Effects of their actions should be readily apparent to them.

However, this design principle also addresses another level of interaction, namely that of the conversation. It allows humans and machines to build an adaptive learning organization, where humans and machines can learn from each other. The obtained knowledge could lead to a change in behavior (of the human or the machine), which should take effect accordingly.

Participatory

Human beings should be able to participate in the decision-making of an HCS. Participatory design is part of the holistic integration of human beings and machines on an equal footing. It does not mean that all decisions are made by people. But, certain key decisions are made together with others (humans and machines).

A participatory system allows human beings to become designers of their human-machine collaboration. It reinforces them in their feeling of being in control of the HCS, and it gives them the opportunity to take the lead.

Consensus Oriented

Participants in HCSs may have different ideals, goals and intentions. In order for collaboration to take place, an exchange of their subjective conceptions is needed for acquiring a mutual agreement and consensus. The principle of consensus-oriented design is about actively supporting this process. Key elements of this design principle are conversation and social cohesion.

In terms of URANOS, finding a consensus means that participants must be able to converse about their goals and intentions first. This happens on the level of the conversation loop. Finding a consensus among human beings also involves mutual respect and empathy. The design must ensure that these aspects are supported on the holistic level by the social cohesion loop.

Effectiveness/Efficiency

This principle focuses on two interrelated requirements: (1) Effectiveness, where system outcomes should be useful for human beings; and (2) efficiency, stating that these outcomes are produced at reasonable costs.

Human-machine collaboration must be performed effectively. The result of that collaboration should correspond as closely as possible to the mutually agreed goals. It also includes how quickly and effectively a system can respond to changing needs. This correlates with the principle of adaptivity.

Further, this principle also covers the sustainable use of natural resources and the protection of a human's environment. Efficiency in this sense helps HCSs to reduce the bio-costs of humans (Geoghegan & Pangaro, 2008), and minimizes wasting of natural resources.

Transparency

In HCSs, decision-making and its enforcement should be comprehensible and achieved legally. Participants affected by the enforcement should be able to easily access the information and regulations that led to the decisions. This leads to transparency and enables participants to learn from their behavior and the provoked effects.

Accountability

The principle of accountability means that participants are liable for their activities according to their roles (e.g. designers, users). Generally, participants are accountable to those who are affected by their decisions and actions (UNESCAP, 2009).

Each participant must be aware of his accountability. Here, local and international law must be considered. The system should provide appropriate information to participants. By means of appropriate warnings, responsibilities can be transferred partially from designers to users.

Example: In many states, technical systems are not legally accountable. Therefore, often, the designer or the user is liable if a technical system fails or endangers human life. This is a big challenge, for instance, in the development of self-driving cars.

MODEL FOR HUMAN-MACHINE COLLABORATION

In our approach to human-centered system design, we focus on the holistic integration of human and machine. Our model allows to integrate human skills and values, making them accessible to the technical system, similarly to the way they are accessible to humans in human-to-human interaction. Values, such as autonomy, freedom of choice and appreciation of their work, leads to human development and accomplishment. This approach reinforces the human being in his feeling of being in control of his life experience in a world of smart technologies. It could also help to reduce human bio-costs like stress, job fears, etc.

Our model for human-machine collaboration is made of three main entities: the human, the machine and the interface between them. In this section, we describe the dynamics between humans and machines, and present the infrastructure that is needed to empower the human-machine collaboration.

Humans

We propose to use the *body-mind continuum* to describe humans. In this context, humans are treated as enactive entities. That is, they are not simply handled as mechanical or information processing systems, but as holistic and social beings. Holistic, because the entanglement of their body and mind leads to an inseparable bond, which constitutes their uniqueness and singularity. And social, because they are not standalone organisms, but are part of a collective in a physical, informational and socio-cultural environment.

The dynamics between human beings and their environment is the starting point to integrate them into HCSs. On the one hand, it is a suitable humanistic integration with machines, leading to a human-machine symbiosis. On the other hand, it constitutes an integration into the socio-cultural environment, which is empowered by HCSs.

Machines

Machines are artificial, man-made systems that are built to fulfill a certain purpose. The term "machine" includes pure mechanical, computerized systems and pure computing systems. Pure mechanical systems will be integrated into HCSs as first-order systems. In this case, the design of the interaction loop plays the crucial role. It determines the accessibility of those machines, enabling other entities to use them.

Computerized machines also encompass perceptual control loops. Sensors collect data, which are then evaluated by computer programs. Simple systems work on statically implemented rules, which lead to actions in the physical environment (e.g. thermostat regulating temperature in a room). Learning and intelligent systems have a certain autonomy. They try to follow complex goals themselves, by making decisions autonomously within a defined range. Hence, we refer to such systems as *smart machines*. Smart machines are integrated in HCSs as second-order systems.

In this model, software of any kind is referred to as a *cyber entity* and exists within *cyber space*. This space includes both static program structures, as well as highly dynamic, self-configuring and self-programming structures.

Human-Machine Integration

In this case, humans and machines are integrated on equal footing. They are closely interconnected, envisaging different forms of human-machine interactions. There are at least two connecting loops between machines and

Figure 2. Human-machine integration means to connect human beings on all pos-sible planes with machines through a human-machine interface (HMI)

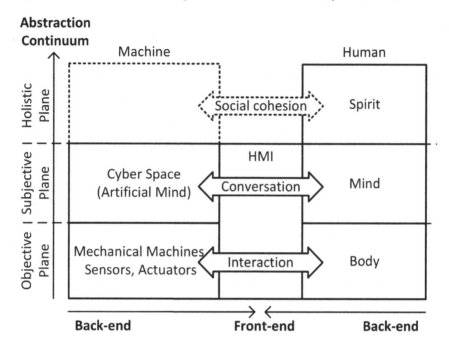

humans: interaction loops and conversation loops (Figure 2). In the future, social cohesion loops will become important as soon as enactive machines are invented.

Human-Machine Interface

Humans and machines are connected via an interface, called the *human-machine interface* (HMI). This interface plays a central role in the integration of humans and machines, as it separates the human from the machine interior and facilitates physical interaction, conversation and social cohesion between them. In this context, separation means that human and machine are decoupled from each other in space and time. From a design point of view, they can then be considered as two distinct entities, which are interconnected on each abstraction plane by a feedback loop.

In the case of interaction between two or more machines, we would rather speak of machine-to-machine interfaces (M2MI). For simplicity reasons, we use the term HMI, being aware that the counterpart of a machine may be a human being or another machine.

Interaction Loops

Physical interactions between humans and machines are represented by interaction loops. Here, humans participate with their physical body and interact with the sensors and actuators of the machine.

Holistic integration of human beings into HCS means to address as many human senses as possible for interaction. In classical HMI design, it is mostly the visual sense of the human being that is taken into account. Other senses, such as hearing, feeling and smelling, are not addressed consciously enough. We propose to integrate them as far as possible to give people a better sense of interaction.

Example: In classical systems an HMI includes some peripheral devices (keyboard, mouse and display) and software implementing a graphical user interface (GUI). In intelligent and pervasive systems, the HMI is much more extensive. Sensors and actuators, which are in contact with the human body, are part of the HMI.

Conversation Loops

Conversation is about exchanging knowledge between humans and smart machines. The conversation process allows an entity (human or machine) to observe its opponent, to interpret their behavior and to react accordingly. For instance, if some of the results of a human-machine collaboration don't meet the requirements as anticipated, a conversation can be launched. The smart machine observes the instructions of a human user, trying to understand and finally reproduce/reflect these instructions (or vice versa when humans learn from smart machines).

In contrast to classical machine learning, where learning is limited to some selected topics and parameters, conversation allows humans and smart machines to build an adaptive learning organization, which is unlimited in terms of conversation topics. Whenever ambiguities arise in the collaboration, it will be handled by an appropriate conversation. Both sides, human and machine, can initiate such conversations. In this sense, conversation enables participants to actively design their collaboration. Users and machines become designers.

Example: Conversation with humans can be realized through classical HMI components like touch screens. In such setups the screen can be seen as a "white board", where human and machine meet each other while visualizing, manipulating and exchanging their goals, models and ideas. A more comprehensive conversation can be realized with the inclusion of other sensors and actuators available, such as cameras, sound etc.

System Governance

An HCS acts as a governance system managing and supporting human activities. Governance in this sense is understood as a *"decision-making and decision implementing process"* so that stable organizations can arise and persist (UNESCAP, 2009).

As shown in Figure 3, governance is performed in two dimensions. The vertical dimension expresses the it-referenced interaction, where a controlling system (upper level) steers the controlled systems (lower levels). And the horizontal dimension addresses the conversation loop between two entities participating in a conversation.

Figure 3. System governance covers the internal control loops (vertical interactions) and the interactions between human and machine (horizontal interactions)

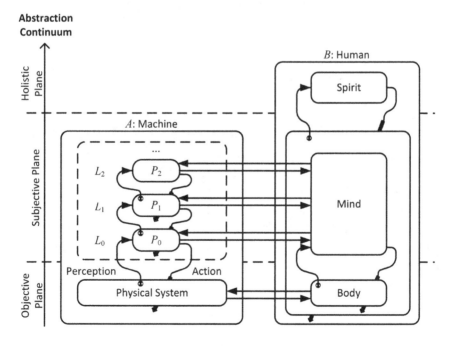

Control

Smart machines are complex control systems. The control is divided into different control levels, each one providing corresponding processes (Figure 3). The lowest control level L_0 contains the controlling process P_0, which measures physical quantities and directly controls actions in the physical environment. As a goal oriented subsystem, P_0 receives its goals from the parent control system P_1. This subsystem measures occurrences in P_0 and adjusts the goals for P_0. This means that, in general, upper control systems divide high level goals into smaller goals, which are then pursued by underlying systems.

Conversation

Each control subsystem P_x of entity A is connected horizontally to some equivalent subsystem of entity B (Figure 3). The set of all horizontal interactions on the subjective plane forms a complex conversation loop. Here, conversation between A and B could involve all control levels. For example, the exchange of new methods over P_1 (the "how") can trigger the exchange of new goals on P_2 (the "why").

Generally speaking, conversation encompasses three levels: L_x handing the "how", L_{x+1} providing the "why" and L_{x-1} denoting a model facility where the subjectivity is embodied and verified. In the sense of Paskian Environments each control level can serve as a model facility for the upper levels (Pask, 1975, Pangaro, 2016). This even holds for the physical level that maintains a concrete physical model of P_0.

Modeling Dimensions

A dedicated system organization helps to manage the increase in structural complexity. In classical software architecture the 3-layered architecture is very common to distinguish between back-end and front-end components (Lemberger & Morel, 2012). In embedded system architecture, the focus is more on the hardware abstraction and implementation of hardware-independent applications. The model for human-machine collaboration comprises both approaches. It is made of two main spectra: the *abstraction continuum* expressing the level of abstraction, and the *closeness* towards humans (Figure 4, Hadorn et al., 2016b).

Figure 4. The abstraction continuum and the closeness to human beings are the two modeling dimensions of a HCS

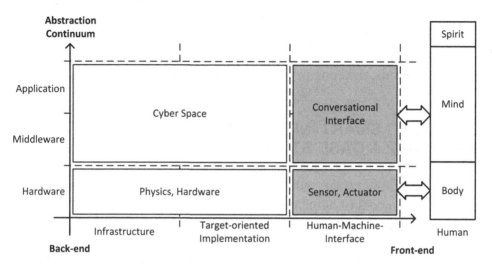

Abstraction Continuum

The first dimension corresponds to the abstraction continuum and describes the level of abstraction. It is divided into three areas: the *hardware*, the *middleware* and the *application*. The hardware encompasses all physical components and physical processes of a system. The middleware is used to abstract the hardware and to provide a hardware-independent interface for applications. Middleware and applications comprise dedicated software components for information processing and decision-making.

Closeness to Human

The second dimension reflects the need to distinguish between back-end and front-end components. It describes the closeness towards the human, and is split into three areas: the *infrastructure*, the *target-oriented implementation* and the *human-machine interface* (HMI). The infrastructure of a system comprises any components that operate in the background (e.g. physical infrastructure, data base, coordination media). Target-oriented implementation includes all components that have been designed for a particular purpose. In software engineering this is often called the "business logic layer" or "service layer". The HMI encompasses all components that are in direct contact with humans. It is the front end of a machine and includes physical and cyber entities alike.

Example: The HMI of a ticketing machine may encompass a physical and a graphical user interface (GUI) to interact with human users. Hardware buttons and a touch screen allow human beings to interact physically with the machine. The GUI is made of cyber entities (software) and allows users and the ticketing machine to exchange information, like destinations, ticketing prices and a timetable.

DESIGNING SMART INDUSTRIAL MACHINES: A CASE STUDY

We aim to present a smart industrial machine design, which is derived from the proposed model of human-machine collaboration. Rather than focusing on a specific application, we want to introduce a framework that is usable for various cyber-physical applications in industrial environments. It provides a generic infrastructure for conversation and for the management of knowledge.

The design mainly focuses on the principles of adaptivity, responsiveness, participation, transparency and consensus-oriented design. Other principles may be added depending on concrete applications.

This section first gives an introduction to smart industrial machines (SIMs). Then, it addresses control and structural layering of their design. And finally, it presents a concrete architecture of a SIM kernel, that allows the implementation of a SIM in hardware and software.

Smart Industrial Machines

We refer to industrial machines as systems used in the secondary sector of the economy, basically to transform raw or intermediate materials into goods, like manufacturing bread from flour or building cars from metal. In the third industrial revolution, many of the manual tasks are automated. Gradually, production processes are optimized by computer-controlled machines, called CNC[2] machines. Furthermore, new processes are developed, which would not be possible without CNC machines, such as additive manufacturing and 3d printing (Naboni & Paoletti, 2015).

Recently, strategies and ideas have been published for the fourth industrial revolution, which provides new production optimization and opportunities. The driving force is the digitalization of society, which puts new demands on production facilities. One vision refers to intelligent production facilities, called *smart factories*. Here, "human, machines and resources will communicate with each other as naturally as in a social network" (Kagermann, Wahlster

& Helbig, 2013). In contrast to classical factories, smart factories enable a fully automated but individualized and customized production. Goods choose their own manufacturing process autonomously throughout the smart factory depending on the factory's load and customer requirements.

Example: A smart automotive factory allows to individualize cars. This goes far beyond choosing from a predefined set of possibilities, like different colors or motor powers. It allows, for instance to add an individually designed interior, as something that has never been ordered before. The factory tries to manufacture this car interior autonomously according to its specification. Therefore, many parameters are considered, such as time of delivery, quality, knowhow, energy consumption, factory load, waste, etc.

In this case study, we address a new generation of human-centered machines for industries, called *smart industrial machines* (SIMs), which fit into these smart factories. Their particular feature is that they are able to collaborate with human beings and other SIMs to a great extent (Hadorn, 2014b).

Example: Producing a fully individualized interior of a car may need novel manufacturing processes. This means, that the factory needs new techniques, skills or knowhow to produce these parts. This knowledge is first possessed by human operators. To make this knowledge usable for smart factories, it must be shared with the SIMs. This happens through conversation, where humans and SIMs exchange their knowledge in order to find a good solution (a shared goal) to manufacture novel parts. In this context, human and SIM work together as a team.

Manufacturing Processes

There is a wide range of manufacturing processes transforming resources to goods. The four important classes are:

- Physical or chemical transformations, like heating, melting, casting.
- Cutting processes, like milling, turning, grinding.
- Additive processes, like welding, surface coating, 3d printing.
- Assembling of parts into a product, wiring, casing.

An item, which is processed in such a process is called a *workpiece*. A manufacturing process requires the control of physical parameters to systematically transform the workpiece. In many cases, a CNC machine must move a tool or instrument relative to the workpiece. Here, parameters like position, speed and acceleration must be controlled. This principle of manufacturing is also subject to a SIM.

Example: A CNC drilling machine has to drill four holes into a plate. To make this process run automatically, it needs an appropriate machining program. This consists of a sequential operation plan, which contains corresponding movements and commands to control axes and other actuators, like coolant valves and the tool spindle. Nowadays, the standardized G-Code programming language is used to express such a machining program, cf. EIA Standard RS-274-D (Electronic Industries Association, 1979). Running this program in the CNC, the four holes are drilled accordingly.

System Learning

The learning process of SIMs is a combination of self-learning (learning by doing) and conversation with human beings and machines. Self-learning can be applied to optimize manufacturing processes through a closed control loop. It is based on observation and reasoning which leads to the adaptation of the process workflows and parameters. But, self-learning is an insufficient approach to learning novel manufacturing concepts.

SIMs are able to enter into a conversation with humans or other machines, enabling them to exchange manufacturing knowledge. Participants of the conversation learn how to manufacture new products. This includes, besides concrete production instructions, technological knowledge and situational behavior (Hadorn, 2014b).

Example: A CNC drilling machine might be able to optimize the feed and speed of the drill autonomously according to the spindle load, drill force and heat. This can be achieved by self-learning algorithms. But the machine cannot learn by itself how to use an unknown tool. If the operator inserts a milling tool the first time, the machine has to learn what it is and how to use it. This knowledge is exchanged through conversation.

Levels of Control

SIMs are intelligent control systems, which manage the production processes at different levels. On the one hand, this includes the operational control of the process. On the other hand, strategic decisions of the smart factory must be considered, like resource-saving or cost-reducing manufacturing. To design such systems, an appropriate control model is needed, which clearly divides and describes each control level.

The model for human-machine collaboration divides the decision-making and control into different levels of control. In principle, the number of levels is not limited. But, the design for human-machine-conversation should be easy to understand. It should follow a natural control grading. In this design approach, we propose to use five levels of control (Figure 5).

Figure 5. Five levels of control, each one connected to the human being as part of the conversation loop (Inspired by complex industrial process control systems, Sanz, 2010).

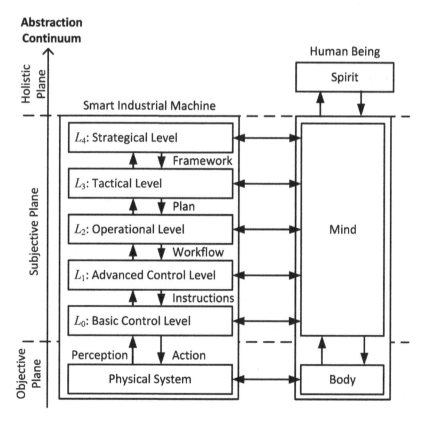

Upper levels deal with high-level goals, such as strategies and tactics. These goals are broken down from level to level into smaller targets. The lowest levels focus on concrete actions which are then executed in the physical environment.

Real-Time Control

The first level, L_0, deals with basic control issues like motion control. It measures physical quantities and directly controls the actuators, like motors and pistons. The closed control loop at this level is very responsive. Depending on the application, it is necessary to have cycle times of less than one millisecond.

The advanced control level, L_1, receives a complex workflow explaining how to accomplish a manufacturing task. Its job is to process the workflow and pass single instructions to L_0. Often, L_0 and L_1 are implemented in real-time embedded systems, like a CNC control unit.

Example: In the context of industrial machines, the control level L_0 encompasses a programmable logic controller (PLC) and a motion controller (MC). The PLC is a general control system, which is constantly monitoring inputs, making decisions and setting outputs in order to control the states of actuators. In contrast, the MC is a real-time system dedicated to steering servomotors towards the predefined target position. In the case of CNC machines, L_1 constitutes the NC-kernel handling instruction for complex geometric tool path movements. Such instructions could lead to coordinated complex movements of several servo motor (axes). Both levels, L_0 and L_1, are implemented in CNC machines as real-time systems.

High-Level Control

Besides the levels L_0 and L_1, SIMs also involve control mechanisms on a higher level. They enable the machine to act more autonomously on complex tasks considering strategical and tactical goals. Three levels of control are distinguished: operational, tactical and strategic.

The operational level, L_2, composes single operations into a workflow. This workflow reflects the subjective manufacturing model, including how the machine would like to collaborate with human beings and other machines. The workflow, as an outcome of L_2, is executed and processed by the underlying level L_1.

The next level, L_3, manages the tactical approach to achieving a common goal. At this level, different tactical approaches are compared and tested against each other. The results are rules and rough procedures to be respected by L_2 in order to generate a specific workflow.

On the strategic level L_4, superordinate goals are determined for the human-machine collaboration and the manufacturing processes. The outcomes are general conditions and rules (framework), from which tactical approaches are derived at the level of L_3.

Example: With SIMs, control levels L_2, L_3 and L_4 can be implemented in a non-real-time computing environment. The operational level, L_2, manages the process workflow and composes NC-programs. The tactical L_3 and strategic L_4 levels manage production strategies that help to optimize the manufacturing process holistically, such as overall speed optimization or energy consumption.

Conversation Process

In a conversation process, several aspects can be exchanged between machines and human beings, like novel manufacturing concepts, agreements, disagreements or misunderstandings about their collaboration. This conversation process can happen on all five control levels. For instance, a human operator disagrees with a generated workflow. He tries to convey at the operational level what needs to be adapted from his point of view (how). At the tactical level, he can additionally explain his motives and goals (why). The SIM adapts its internal model at both levels.

In turn, the machine can also request information through appropriate demands to close knowledge gaps in its subjective model. After teaching the machine, the human being gets direct feedback through the customized workflow. He can then verify if the machine has understood his explanations. The conversation ends with mutual consent. Finally, the machine has learned new circumstances from a human being. Collaboration can now enter the next stage on a deeper control level. This interplay is repeated until an effective physical collaboration between participants takes place. This principle also works if the human being learns from the SIM. In this case, the operator's lack of knowledge is closed by information provided by the machine.

The conversation can happen anytime - before, during or after a production process. Both the machine and the human being can intervene and try to resolve their differences through conversation at the appropriate levels. For instance, a human operator can intervene and teach the machine how to improve the process refining the current manufacturing concepts. The conversation ends when both human being and machine agree on the adapted concepts.

The knowledge gained from conversation is stored in relation to the situation it learned. The situation includes context information, such as "who taught the concepts?", "what was the workpiece being manufactured?" or "what was the production strategy (e.g. economic, ecologic or express production)?" (Hadorn, 2014b). The knowledge gained can also be abstracted and generalized by conversation. For instance, the machine can ask a human if a learned concept applies only to this situation, or if it is rather a general issue. This allows the machine to become more and more autonomous.

Structural Layering

The design is structured in the two proposed dimensions, abstraction continuum and closeness towards the human (or exterior). This results in a system architecture which includes physical and cyber domains, as well as interfaces towards humans or other machines (Hadorn, Courant & Hirsbrunner, 2016a; Hadorn et al. 2016b).

Physical Domain

In the physical domain, SIMs consist of three types of components: the *physical infrastructure*, the *mechanical devices* and the *mechanical ergonomics*.

The physical infrastructure (Figure 6a) works as a supporting facility for any kind of hardware. It encompasses, among other things, electrical wiring and piping for fluid and air.

Mechanical devices (Figure 6b) are target implementations and artifacts designed for specific purposes. For instance, a motor cooling system is designed to keep the motor temperature stable.

Mechanical ergonomics (Figure 6c) are implementations interacting directly with the human-body. They can be seen as physical HMIs, like displays, buttons, door handles or windows.

Cyber Domain

The cyber domain covers cyber entities like software components, control processes, and conversational interfaces. Here, software systems do not necessarily run on a single hardware platform. They can also be realized as a distributed computing system. The cyber domain is structured into four components: the *ubiquitous hardware abstraction layer* (UHAL), the *per-*

vasive middleware layer (PeMiL), the *pervasive service layer* (PeSeL), and the *smart application layer* (SAL).

The UHAL interfaces with the physical domain (Figure 6d). This layer encompasses operation systems, drivers and services that handle infrastructure and hardware devices. The main purpose of this layer is to unify and homogenize the heterogeneous nature of devices. This allows higher level systems to deal more easily with changing hardware settings.

The PeMiL comprises the artificial mind of the SIM (Figure 6e). Here, the five levels of control manage the dynamic and adaptive behavior. It also consists of semantic processing networks designed to process and store information (knowledge).

The PeSeL implements target-oriented services towards an HMI (Figure 6f). In software engineering, this layer is often referred to as the business logic layer.

The SAL is part of the conversational interface implementing the system's front-end (Figure 6g). Its primary concern is direct conversation with human beings. In addition to the graphical user interfaces (GUI), it includes other visual or sound effects.

Figure 6. Structural layering of smart industrial machines, made of (a) a physical infrastructure, (b) a mechanical devices, (c) a mechanical ergonomics, (d) an ubiquitous hardware abstraction layer (UHAL), (e) a pervasive middleware layer (PeMiL), (f) a pervasive service layer (PeSeL), and (g) a smart application layer (SAL)

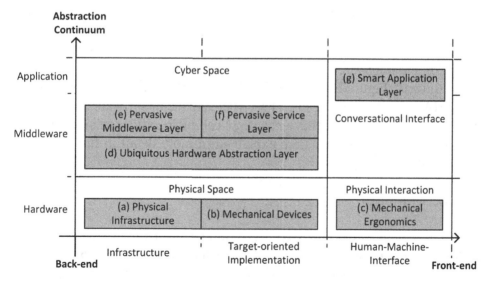

Integration of Smart Devices

The architecture of SIMs goes beyond the centralized management of hardware devices, as realized in classical industrial machines. SIMs are also able to handle intelligent and autonomous devices which have their own integrated control system. Such devices are referred to as *smart devices* (Hadorn et al., 2016a).

Although a smart device receives control instructions from the machine control, these instructions are independently and autonomously executed and monitored by the device. Only status information and events are returned as feedback to the machine control. Thus, communication between the machine control and the devices is reduced to a minimum.

Ideally, smart devices are automatically detected and configured by the SIM. This behavior is referred to as *self-configuration*[3]. It allows to use new smart devices without large manual integration efforts. For this purpose, the smart device provides semantic device information. This information can be used by the higher control levels to optimally integrate these devices into the production process. In this context, the self-configuration also encompasses the reconfiguration and adaptation of the manufacturing processes (Hadorn et al., 2016a).

Architecture of Smart Machine Kernel

As part of the SIM design, we propose an application-independent kernel for these machines. The purpose of this kernel is to accommodate the perceived and constructed subjective reality of SIMs. Therefore, the architecture encompasses mainly software components, and in particular it describes the design of a middleware.

As shown in Figure 7, the architecture of the kernel includes several layers, like UHAL, PeMiL and PeSeL. The kernel is made of software components implementing dynamical behavior and application-specific extensions through plug-ins. These components are explained in more detail in the following paragraphs:

Device Manager

The *device manager* belongs to the UHAL and manages all hardware devices, actuators and sensors of a machine. This includes among other things, input and output devices allowing physical interactions with human beings.

Figure 7. Architecture of a SIM kernel; the kernel integrates hardware through the ubiquitous hardware abstraction layer (UHAL) and conversation participant through the conversational services (PeSeL). The dynamic and adaptive behavior is achieved through the semantic processing network, structured by five control levels.

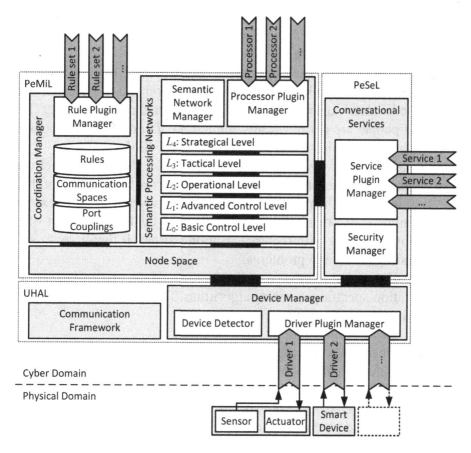

In the dynamic world of HCSs, new hardware devices are automatically detected and configured. The *device detector* is the key player of this self-configuring behavior of SIMs, recognizing devices, be they purely mechanical or smart devices. It is also responsible for setting up the necessary infrastructure, so that these devices are properly integrated. This includes dynamic loading of device drivers, which provide a homogeneous interface and communication protocol towards the upper layers.

Semantic Processing Network

The actual decision-making and control takes place in a *semantic processing network*. It consists of processing nodes, which transform and archive information, and combine it with other information building knowledge. Instructions are the output of the network. They are transmitted to actuators, which are able to execute them.

The network is constructed in the five control levels. L_0 and L_1 are real-time capable networks able to control hardware and smart devices in real-time. These levels are also responsible for human and machine safety. They ensure that people are not physically injured. L_2, L_3 and L_4 are responsible for operational, tactical and strategic control of the SIM.

The *semantic network manager* is used to validate the semantic network. If discrepancies are detected, this manager first tries to solve the problem itself. But, it also has the possibility to initiate a conversation with external partners (humans or other machines) making the conflict a subject of the conversation. Together with the conversation partner, it then tries to solve the outstanding issues and problems.

The *processor plug-in manager* allows to extend the processing network with application-specific processing algorithms. They are dynamically loaded on demand as processing nodes.

Example: A camera feeds its video streams into the processing network. Appropriate signal processing, such as filtering and pattern recognition, will be provided to the kernel through a plug-in. Once the camera is detected (UHAL), the network is extended with desired processing nodes provided by this plug-in.

Node Space

Within the SIM kernel, there is a huge amount of software objects representing the subjective reality, which is perceived and acquired by the machine. These objects, like rules, processing nodes, data nodes and relations, are managed in a *node space*. Its main function is to persist this subjective reality. Relational or object-oriented databases could serve as a concrete implementation.

Coordination Manager

The *coordination manager* is in charge of managing and applying rules. Events, like the detection of new devices, trigger rules, which then take the appropriate actions in the system. Amongst other things, they are used for building and maintaining the semantic processing network.

The coordination manager also mediates communication spaces between the entities. On one side, it manages the communication channels within the semantic processing networks. But, it also manages the communication channels to external entities, like TCP-IP connections to conversation partners.

Application-specific rules and regulations can be provided as plug-ins. The *rule plug-in manager* administers these plug-ins.

Example: The detection of a recently plugged in camera causes an event that triggers certain rules. The actions defined within these rules build and change the semantic processing network. This may include processing methods to process the video stream accordingly. But it could also involve the change of purely semantic links.

Conversational Services

Conversational services allow conversational partners to interact with the machine and to exchange their models, concepts, intentions and ideas. They can be seen as a "gateway" to access certain parts of the semantic processing network, its data and processes.

Application-specific services are managed by the *service plug-in manager*. According to the needs of the external conversation partner services are loaded dynamically.

The *security manager* plays an important role managing services. It ensures that unauthorized entities cannot cause any harm. People and machines have to authenticate in order to be authorized to use conversational services. It also ensures security on the level of the provided data. Each entity receives its granted information depending on its permission role.

Example: A smart white board is used as part of a conversational interface between a machine and human beings. This board can be seen as a shared space between them allowing to exchange their ideas and concepts. Similarly to human beings, the machine observers and reacts up on the changing content in relation to a previously chosen conversation topic. On the machine side, the services for observation and drawing are guarded by the security manager. It prevents the release of classified information to unauthorized participants.

Reflection on Design Principles

In this section, we proposed a cyber-physical framework applicable for smart industrial machines. It dynamically implements the behaviors of HCSs providing infrastructure for conversation and management of knowledge. The design meets the principles of adaptivity, responsiveness, participation, transparency and consensus-oriented design.

- **Adaptivity:** It is achieved by coordination based on dynamic rules. As part of the semantic network, rules and their enforcement can be learned by the machine through conversation. By applying such rules, internal structures, like the semantic processing network, are created and adapted to the human's needs. This leads to a highly dynamic behavior of the machine.
- **Responsiveness:** The responsiveness of the system is improved by the different control levels. Each request has its own response time. The real-time control levels L_0 and L_1 react very quickly and within a precisely defined period. This allows to control and monitor movements and safety aspects. Higher control levels may react slowly and unevenly. Depending on the application, the impact of a strategical change is not always immediately apparent.
- **Participatory and Consensus-Oriented:** Through the principle of conversation, SIMs and humans can equally share their models, intentions and goals. This allows on the one hand, that decisions are taken together (participation), and on the other hand, it enables the humans and SIMs to find a consensus in conflicting situations.
- **Transparency:** This is accomplished by the disclosure of decision-making processes. The semantic processing network, which leads to decisions and thus actions, is made accessible and transparent by appropriate monitoring services.

CONCLUSION

This chapter focused on human-centered systems (HCSs). They differ from user-centered systems in that human beings are put in the center of the design and the system processes. Our approach is based on three main aspects. First, human beings must be integrated as holistic and social beings. Second, the design and the system itself must be devoted to human values and help to reduce bio-costs of humans. And finally, an HCS must adapt to changing needs and requirements.

We proposed several design principles, among others, the principles of adaptivity, responsiveness, participation, consensus-oriented behavior and transparency design. The goal of these principles is to guide the design of an HCS preventing frustration and empowering enthusiasm when human beings start to collaborate with that system.

A model for human-machine collaboration was presented. It is based on the three instantiations of URANOS, namely body-mind continuum, integral thinking and cognitive coordination, and it is guided by design principles for human-centered design.

Finally, a design for HCSs was presented, which is derived from the proposed model of human-machine collaboration. It describes a framework that is usable for various cyber-physical applications. It provides a generic infrastructure for conversation and management of knowledge. In this context, the concrete example of smart industrial machines (SIMs) is introduced. The outstanding feature of these machines is that they form an adaptive learning organization with human beings. This means, that it can dynamically learn from human beings how to manufacture new products. And conversely, it can train human operators on how to operate the machine in order to fulfill changing manufacturing requirements.

HCSs have great potential to bring the digitalization of the world decisively forward. With an integral and holistic approach, people and their natural and socio-cultural environment are sustainably taken into account. This will bring the following benefits:

- Due to conversation, HCSs can actively learn new behavior and concepts from human beings. This allows to respond quickly to new needs and requirements without expensive reconfiguration and reprogramming.
- The HCS can give gained knowledge back to human beings, supporting them in their work and individual learning processes.

- HCS increases the chance of successful collaboration, because it enables the participants (humans and machines) to reach a shared agreement of common understanding.
- The human-centered design reduces the bio costs of humans and reinforces the human being in his feeling of being in control of his life experience.
- Finally, human-centered design allows to build super intelligent systems, where machines are responsible for automation and continuity, and human beings contribute their enactive capabilities (consciousness, cre-adaption and individuation).

We are convinced that in the near future human-centered and sustainable system design will gain in relevance.

REFERENCES

Cooley, M. (2008). On Human-Machine Symbiosis. In Cognition, Communication and Interaction: Transdisciplinary Perspectives on Interactive Technology (pp. 457-485). London, UK: Springer. doi:10.1007/978-1-84628-927-9_26

Electronic Industries Association. (1979). *EIA Standard RS-274-D Interchangeable Variable Block Data Format for Positioning, Contouring, and Contouring/Positioning Numerically Controlled Machines*. Washington, DC: Electronic Industries Association.

Gasson, S. (2003). Human-centered vs. user-centered approaches to information system design. *Journal of Information Technology Theory and Application*, 5(2), 29–46.

Geoghegan, M. C., & Pangaro, P. (2009). Design for a Self-regenerating Organization. *International Journal of General Systems*, 38(2), 155–173. doi:10.1080/03081070802633700

Gill, K. S. (1996). The Foundations of Human-centred Systems. In K. S. Gill (Ed.), *Human Machine Symbiosis: The Foundations of Human-centred Systems Design* (pp. 1–68). London, UK: Springer. doi:10.1007/978-1-4471-3247-9_1

Gill, K. S., Funston, T., Thrope, J., Hijitaka, M., & Gotze, J. (1993). Individuals, culture and the design of information systems. In C. Beardon & D. Whitehouse (Eds.), *Computers and Society* (pp. 76–90). Oxford, UK: Intellect Books.

Hadorn, B. (2014b). *Smart Grinding Maschine - Innovation Memorandum* (Internal White Paper). Steffisburg, Switzerland: Innovation Electronics and Software, Studer.

Hadorn, B., Courant, M., & Hirsbrunner, B. (2015b). Holistic Integration of Enactive Entities into Cyber Physical Systems. *2nd IEEE International Conference on Cybernetics, CYBCONF 2015*. Gdynia, Poland: IEEE. doi:10.1109/CYBConf.2015.7175947

Hadorn, B., Courant, M., & Hirsbrunner, B. (2016b). *Towards Human-Centered Cyber Physical Systems: A Modeling Approach*. Fribourg, Switzerland: University of Fribourg.

Hadorn, B., Josi, C., Zwahlen, R., Lüthi, M., Abbühl, M., & Albertin, R. (2016a). *Plug and Produce for Smart Tooling Machines* (Internal White Paper). Steffisburg, Switzerland: Innovation Electronics and Software, Studer.

Hüther, G. (2012). Learning enthusiastically. A conversation with Prof. Dr. Gerald Hüther. *Televizion, 25*, 14–15.

Hüther, G. (2016, June 28). *Begeisterung*. Retrieved from http://www.gerald-huether.de/populaer/veroeffentlichungen-von-gerald-huether/texte/begeisterung-gerald-huether/

Jaimes, A., Gatica-Perez, D., Sebe, N. & Huang, T. S. (2007). Human-centered Computing: Toward a Human Revolution. *IEEE Computer, 40*(5), 30-34.

Kagermann, H., Wahlster, W. & Helbig, J. (2013). *Securing the Future of German Manufacturing Industry: Recommendations for Implementing the Strategic Initiative INDUSTRIE 4.0, Final Report of the Industrie 4.0 Working Group*. Berlin, Germany: Forschungsunion im Stifterverband für die Deutsche Wirtschaft e.V.

Lemberger, P. P., & Morel, M. (2012). *Managing Complexity of Information Systems: The value of simplicity*. London, UK: John Wiley & Sons, Inc. doi:10.1002/9781118562017

Naboni, R., & Paoletti, I. (2015). *Advanced Customization in Architectural Design and Construction* (1st ed.). Springer International Publishing. doi:10.1007/978-3-319-04423-1

Pangaro, P. (2016, July 5). *Paskian Environments with Paul Pangaro*. Retrieved from http://www.haque.co.uk/paskianenvironments.php

Pask, G. (1975). *Conversation, Cognition and Learning: A Cybernetic Theory and Methodology*. New York, NY: Elsevier Publishing Company.

Sanz, R. (2010, February 15). Intelligence, Control and the Artificial Mind. *PerAda Magazine, 2010*, 1–3.

Schwartz, S. H. (2006). *Basic Human Values: An Overview*. Jerusalem, Israel: The Hebrew University of Jerusalem.

United Nations Economic and Social Commission for Asia and the Pacific. (2009). *What is Good Governance?* Retrieved from http://www.unescap.org/resources/what-good-governance

Weijers, D. (2016). Hedonism. *The Internet Encyclopedia of Philosophy*. Retrieved from http://www.iep.utm.edu/hedonism

ENDNOTES

[1]   Some of the design principles are correlated with the principles of good governance (UNESCAP, 2009). They are adapted to human-centered design and human-machine collaboration.

[2]   Computerized Numerical Control

[3]   In context of smart factories and the fourth industrial revolution, this is also referred to as "plug and produce".

Conclusion

INTRODUCTION

Many research disciplines are confronted with complex and non-linear systems. Generic system models offer a common language to understand such systems, and encourage interdisciplinary research among different domains, such as computer science, biology and sociology.

The generic system model URANOS is not aligned to any particular discipline, but potentially addresses the entire field of knowledge. It provides a framework that helps to build integral systems in different domains of science and engineering. Therefore, it combines various epistemological standpoints and their corresponding realities into a wholeness. Currently, the three fundamental standpoints of objectivism, subjectivism and holism are used to describe complex and non-linear systems. The model focuses on dynamics and aspects emerging from each standpoint and shows how they are interrelated with each other. Further, it describes how different systems can be combined to form a symbiosis. Finally, URANOS encompasses holistic and systemic features, like consciousness, collaboration and symbiosis from a generic standpoint.

We instantiated URANOS to approach human-centered system design in the framework of ICT. In this context, the methodology of integral thinking and systemic design was used, where human beings (or other living systems) are considered as holistic beings. In this work, several design principles were proposed, which ensure that the design of a system respects human integrity and does not discriminate against human beings in terms of their origin, race, culture, age and sex. The produced system is referred to as *human-centered*, as it can enter into a symbiotic relationship with human beings.

This chapter outlines the conclusion of our research work on generic system modeling and human-centered design. Section "URANOS: A New Cosmology" reviews our generic system model URANOS. Section "URANOS: Human in the Focus" recalls the research on human-centered system design, especially integrating human beings into technical systems. In section "Open Perspectives", new perspectives and open issues are presented, and finally, section "Epilogue" closes this chapter with an epilogue.

URANOS: A NEW COSMOLOGY

URANOS constitutes a new cosmology providing a common and generic understanding of complex and non-linear systems across research and engineering disciplines like complex smart machine and pervasive and human-centered computing. This section summarizes our generic system model, describing the different systemic orders, evolutionary development processes, entity's collaboration and the emerging symbiotic relations with each other. Further, a review is given on URANOS's genericity and its instantiations towards concrete models.

A Holistic Modeling Approach

When speaking of holism, one immediately thinks of describing a system comprehensively, focusing mainly on aspects which emerge from the system as a whole. As a result, one pays less or no attention to details. But, in the evolution of a system, details might lead to new behavior. In this sense, we follow the arguments of E. Morin (1992). It is important to distinguish entities from each other, but at the same time their relationship to one another must be taken into account, so that they can be understood in the context of the whole.

URANOS offers a comprehensive view of the system equally considering the parts and the emerging whole. Various epistemological standpoints are needed to explain the totality of complex and non-linear systems. These standpoints, namely objectivism, subjectivism and holism, are mapped to an abstraction continuum. This leads to abstraction planes, namely the objective, subjective and holistic planes. Each plane describes the reality proposed by the corresponding standpoint.

From an objective standpoint, reality is described as first-order and interactive systems. From this standpoint, systems are addressed mainly by the technical sciences, such as physics, chemistry or biology. Entities, interactions and rules are the objective constructs of URANOS. The continuous change of entities through interactions leads to an evolutionary development process.

This process is limited and regulated through rules. An interactive system can be described by causal effects, chains and feedback loops. In particular, reinforcing and dampening feedback loops affect the growth and stability of a system. Superposition of several feedback loops form very complex circuits, which maintain the system.

Combining objective and subjective standpoints leads to second-order systems, called smart entities. They cover a spectrum of systems, from simple control systems like thermostats to complex living systems like human beings. Many of the aspects emerging from second-order systems are addressed by, among others, computer science, constructive biology, psychology and sociology. A key issue is to involve subjectivity, which arises from the observation of entities through sophisticated processes, referred to as perceptual control loops. These processes are the reason that each smart entity has its own subjective image of the reality, and generates an awareness. Autopoietic systems are also introduced. They are characterized by their operational closure and ability to maintain and to reproduce themselves. These characteristics mainly apply to living systems. An autopoiesis loop connects objective and subjective realities, describing their mutual influence as a closed feedback loop.

Our cosmology also addresses living and social systems, which cannot be described exhaustively by the objective-subjective dualism. A third systemic order is introduced describing such systems from a holistic standpoint. On the corresponding abstraction plane, objective and subjective realities are entangled and must be considered as an inseparable whole, a holistic being. Third-order systems are referred to as enactive entities. In this sense, "enaction" describes a system that gains its knowledge through an incremental learning process based on perception and action (Varela, Thompson & Rosch, 1993). Enactive entities are characterized by three fundamental aspects: the ability to be aware of themselves and their surroundings (consciousness), the ability to adapt their behavior or create new behaviors (cre-adaption), and the ability to differentiate themselves from the environment (individuation).

Collaboration and Symbiosis

URANOS describes the way that two or more entities can work together. This is referred to as collaboration, which goes beyond simple objective interactions. Collaborative entities are connected to each other on all abstraction planes. Collaboration could lead to a symbiotic relationship. In this context, symbiosis is defined as a collaborative entanglement between two or more entities pursuing a common goal, which generates a mutual benefit.

There exist three feedback loops connecting the collaborative entities and maintaining their symbiosis. On the objective plane, entities are coupled through interaction loops, denoting concrete interactions between them, like a physical exchange of energy or matter. On the subjective plane, a conversation loop enables entities to exchange constructs of their subjective realities, like ideas, models and goals. This loop describes a complex interaction between smart entities, which mainly depends on one entity's interpretation of the other's behavior (Pask, 1975; Pangaro, 1989). And on the holistic plane, a social cohesion loop connects exclusively enactive entities allowing them to develop togetherness and collectiveness. Through social cohesion, collaborating entities form a new wholeness. This means, that they have to be considered together in order to understand their behavior.

Symbiosis also happens between an entity and its environment. In this sense, an environment itself can be seen as a complex system. For instance, human beings are connected to their environment on all abstraction planes. On the objective plane, the human body interacts with the physical environment. On the subjective plane, the human mind is connected to an informational environment and finally on the holistic plane, they are connected to a socio-cultural environment.

System Development

In addition to the evolutionary process described from the objective standpoint, URANOS also addresses a systemic development process leading to complexity. It describes how new dynamics and systemic aspects emerge or disappear on the different abstraction planes while a system grows or shrinks in complexity.

During its lifetime, a system can pass through several development stages. Our cosmology distinguishes between two kinds of stages: morphogenesis and homeostasis. Morphogenesis describes development stages that are characterized by growth and differentiation. Homeostasis, on the other hand, characterizes stages which promote order, stability and constancy.

There are two opposing forces that affect and drive this development process: the urge for self-organization, which leads to order and structure in the system, and entropic drift, which provokes disorder and change.

Genericity

URANOS is a generic and abstract framework to help to understand systems from different epistemological standpoints. It is not an all-in-one model suitable for every imaginable purpose. As an abstract framework, it must be instantiated, adapted and refined for concrete research and engineering cases.

In three concrete instantiations, we demonstrated how URANOS can be derived and instantiated towards a concrete use case. The first instantiation describes human beings as holistic and spiritual beings based on a body-mind continuum. Here, humans are comprehensively considered within complex, technical and social systems. In a second instantiation, a model for integral thinking is proposed. The model is based on the AQAL-model (Wilber, 2007) which has been extended with the perspective of explicit dynamics. And finally, the third instantiation addresses holistic and cognitive coordination processes in the context of multi-agent and cyber-physical systems. Each of these instantiation bears our generic framework at its core, but at the same time has its own specifications.

As a generic framework, URANOS is flexible in terms of extensibility through new systemic orders and epistemological standpoints. This means, that we are not limited to third-order systems. As a possible extension towards a fourth-order system, the concept of a holon can be used. Holons are entities which are simultaneously a wholeness and parts of a larger wholeness. Approaching towards this fourth-order, many open issues and questions still remain.

URANOS: HUMAN IN THE FOCUS

Technologies, like computing and information technology, are invading our daily life to an ever-greater extent. On the one hand, many circumstances are simplified and become more comfortable for humans. On the other hand, issues such as privacy, autonomy and independence are neglected. We aimed to provide an integral and sustainable solution for research and engineering disciplines putting the human in the center of our work.

Human-Centered Approach

Through a concrete case study, we have seen that URANOS can be used to approach towards a human-centered system (HCS) designing proposing a model for humanistic and holistic human-machine collaboration. Human beings, machines and their interactions are considered from each standpoint, which leads to a comprehensive view on complex dynamics, like human-machine symbiosis or socio-cultural interactions. Our approach to design an HCS is based on three main aspects:

First, human beings must be integrated holistically. Based on the body-mind continuum, we showed how human beings can enter into a collaboration with technical systems as holistic and social beings. This means, that the system is designed to treat human beings as individuals, each one having its own subjective view, preferences, skills and socio-cultural backgrounds. This is far from dealing with average users.

Second, the design and the operation of a system must be devoted to human values and help to reduce bio-costs of collaborating humans. The goal is to preserve human dignity and integrity in any human-machine symbiosis.

And third, the system behavior must adapt to the changing needs and requirements of humans and their social communities enabling new human activities to arise. An HCS distinguishes itself from other systems by the way it allows human beings to constantly incorporate their needs, skills and creativity into system processes.

In an HCS, a human being is able to become a designer of his human-machine collaboration. This means, that the human can enter in a design process and actively participate in decision-making processes. We argued that this reinforces his feeling of being in control, and gives him the opportunity to take the lead. Additionally, it enables people to self-realize when working with the system.

Designing for Human Beings

The task of engineers has changed greatly in the last decades. There is an increasing demand for integral and sustainable solutions. This means that in addition to technology issues, psychological, humanistic and socio-cultural aspects also have to be considered. Thus, designing systems becomes more complex and elaborated.

Our model for human-centered system design proposes nine design principles which help researchers and engineers focus on the relevant aspects in their design. These principles are derived from the insights of our generic system modeling and reflect the holistic and integral thinking perspective. The principles are:

1. Devotion to human values;
2. Equality and inclusiveness;
3. Adaptivity;
4. Responsiveness;
5. Participatory design;
6. Consensus oriented behavior;

7. Effectiveness and efficiency;
8. Transparency; and
9. Accountability.

Furthermore, good design mediates the relevance and meaningfulness of a system to its users. And this is one of the most important prerequisites for people that they can develop positive emotions about a system. Design should provoke positive emotions! Current brain research confirms that positive emotions, such as enthusiasm, are crucial for human learning (Hüther, 2012), where negative emotions, like frustration, should be avoided.

Human-Machine Collaboration

Our model of human-machine collaboration handles human beings and machines on equal footing. Between them, an interface separates the human from the machine interior and facilitates physical interaction, conversation and social cohesion between them.

We proposed a two-dimensional model to design human-centered and smart machines. The first dimension addresses the abstraction level, and the second dimension expresses the closeness towards humans, from back-end to front-end. This model describes both, the structural and dynamical aspects, in these two dimensions. Furthermore, a refined control model differentiates control and conversational processes in several control levels. For instance, an HCS could consists of five control levels, basic and advanced control, and operational, tactical and strategical levels. Each of these levels can be connected to human beings forming a complex conversation loop.

Based on the model for human-machine collaboration, our design for HCSs can be used for various cyber-physical applications. This design has been applied to the concrete example of smart industrial machines (SIMs) in the context of smart factories (Kagermann, Wahlster & Helbig, 2013). Their outstanding feature is that they can form an adaptive learning organization with human beings. This means, that the machine can dynamically learn from human beings, and conversely, it can train human beings to operate the machine. As a use case, we have seen a prototype software architecture for SIMs.

OPEN PERSPECTIVES

URANOS offers many interesting perspectives for different research and engineering domains. Maybe one of major contributions of our work is to bring a new world view on reality which encompasses not only physical but also cognitive and abstract aspects. This can be seen as an epistemological step, which could have a great impact on current science and engineering. And beyond, it brings a new unified view of knowledge and matter to our society. This approach is able to infuse in the very depth of commonsense and deeply affects the way we apprehend our reality.

This section presents the most significant perspectives in the area of computer science, system engineering, economics and organizational science. Further, it outlines some possible future research in generic system modeling and human-center system design.

Computer Science

Computing has become increasingly important for our society in recent decades. It develops more and more in the direction of an integral research discipline. In this context, cognitive, psychological and socio-cultural aspects are studied and some are even integrated in current computing models.

With our approach, we can contribute to this community to a great extent. Our model provides a holistic and integral standpoint for developing computing systems taking human beings into account. It opens the possibility of designing adaptive solutions, which are able to individualize their behavior in terms of a human's origin, race, culture, age and sex.

Specifically, disciplines like HCI, and human-centered and pervasive computing could benefit from our work. Instead of replicating human intelligence in a computer system, human beings and computing systems can enter into a conversation, forming an adaptive learning organization. Here, human skills could be made accessible to the computing system, similarly to the way they are accessible to humans in human-to-human interaction.

This will open up new opportunities in their user-centered and human-centered approaches, like personalized, individualized and socio-cultural dependent software solutions. Actually, this kind of human-machine collaboration can be used wherever innovation, creativity, inspiration and well-being and emotions meet automated processes.

Example: Nowadays, many new innovations in industry meet rigid and inflexible production processes. Reconfiguring and reprogramming of these processes is very expensive and requires many specialists who may not be available quickly enough to react to new customer needs in time. This dilemma could be solved by human-centered design. SIMs build with human beings an adaptive learning organization, where the machines are responsible for automation, accuracy and continuity, and where the human brings creativity, inspiration and innovation to the system.

Example: HCS could also be applied to the future of human mobility, where autonomous vehicles share the road with pedestrians and cyclists. In doing so, these systems (and humans) will have to learn massively from each other, so that this can be done well. They must be able to adapt quickly and easily to new situations, be it new vehicles, regulations or laws.

Example: Another potential are intelligent buildings and housing facilities that adapt to the inhabitant. Or even more, where the inhabitant becomes the designer of its automation and determines what he wants or not depending on his daily form. This needs a conversation so that the system can understand what is required in which situation. And this is far from having an app with hundreds of parameters to be set.

We are convinced that integral and generic approaches in computer science could lead to a new revolution in the age of digitalization.

Systemics

Many challenges and problems of our time can only be solved by interdisciplinary collaboration and transdisciplinary perspectives. This requires unified and holistic models, so that problems are understood and solved beyond the limits of research and engineering disciplines and their models. Our systemic approach contributes to building such models, supporting interdisciplinary collaboration. URANOS helps to consider all relevant aspects of a system, be it physical, computational, humanistic or socio-cultural. Therefore, it provides a comprehensive understanding and terminology for researchers and engineers about complex structures and system dynamics.

Further, URANOS allows to bring different and domain specific perspectives into one model. In this context, perspectives are not classified as being right or wrong. Rather, each domain can communicate at eye level with each other. This encourages researchers and engineers to collaborate beyond their different domains, even if their approaches and models are completely different.

Example: One of the major challenges of the upcoming decade will be to stabilize global warming. Already, in order to understand this problem holistically, diverse perspectives and research domains are needed. It is far beyond a physical or a political process. Based on URANOS, a holistic model can help to describe different aspects in one model, like physical, psychological and socio-cultural aspects. It allows understanding the dynamics within and between these aspects, as well as how living and man-made systems are embedded in the changing environment, be it the physical, the informational or the socio-cultural environment.

Economics and Organizational Science

Economy can be seen as a human-centered system, which is interwoven with human societies to a high degree. Human beings are integrated on a natural basis, working together in teams and organizations to pursue common goals.

Our generic approach can contribute to a deeper understanding and a conscious management of organizations. In this context, human beings must be integrated into organizations through the three connecting feedback loops proposed: interaction, conversation and social cohesion. This could lead to integral leadership, and influence the management of human resources, successful team work and communication with business partners. It ensures that human beings, like employees, business partners and customers, are well treated and can enter into collaboration with that organization.

The proposed design principles for HCS also hold when forming an organization. For instance, the principle of participatory design means that each human being becomes a co-designer within that organization and can take part in decision-making processes. Following the approach of human-centeredness could be a door opener for many companies and teams, where today human employees are mostly perceived as an expense.

Example: Fixed and rigid hierarchies are becoming an obstacle for teams to act quickly and proactively, in a world where technological change is still speeding up. Here, well performing teams become more and more important. On the one hand, URANOS can help to democratize companies, meaning to let human beings participate in decision-making processes. On the other hand, it helps to understand and cultivate team spirit and performance.

Future Research

The fact that we have taken this generic approach opens up new opportunities for us to bring digitalization and networking of today's society forward. Rather than following the path of collecting data or exchanging information in a large scale, we proclaim a human-centered approach putting human beings, their society, natural and socio-cultural environments in the center of our design processes. Here, many issues are still unknown and require interdisciplinary collaboration, like a deeper cybernetic understanding of human beings, their psyche and the way they interact with socio-technical systems. Yes, this will lead to the next technological, socio-cultural, philosophical and even existential revolution.

Currently, we look at life as a constitution caused by an endless recursion driven by autopoiesis. Our own existence is trapped in this recursion and this probably hinders our understanding of ourselves in detail. In this context, a deeper epistemological and fundamental study of autopoietic and autogenetic feedback loops is required. For instance, is there a way to express these loops in terms of mathematics or physics? Or, do we have to consider them as a kind of systemic "axiom", a natural phenomenon? To find answers, we need to advance further in the world of complex and non-linear systems.

In parallel, we aim to continue our research on a software platform for human-centered systems, in particular for smart industrial machines (SIMs). This challenging software project, called HumanOS™, mainly focuses on conversation and the associated learning processes of human beings and machines. In this book, we presented an architecture of an adaptive SIM kernel, which is a starting point for this software project. HumanOS™ can be seen as a meta-program producing an autopoietic topology that reflects the behavior learned through conversation and observation. In this sense, the system behavior is not programmed but learned either through conversation with other systems or humans, or through observation and classical machine learning. This allows to use HumanOS™ for different applications and engineering fields as it adapts its "mind" to new situations and topics.

EPILOGUE

Sustainability means to be in a closed and stable feedback loop. As we developed URANOS, we learned to see the world from an integral and generic standpoint. It was amazing to see how far generic theories and models, such as conversation theory, have been evolved in the past century. But, it was also surprising that lots of these works are mostly unknown to mainstream ICT and AI. From our standpoint, technology and design is still far away from being human-centered. There is much to do in this area before an HCS can successfully work together with people. We hope that with this work we contribute to the human-centered initiative. We intend to continue research in this direction, to conceive systems that fit in the natural, social and cultural context of human beings. The world needs a change towards greater sustainability and integral solutions.

REFERENCES

Hüther, G. (2012). Learning enthusiastically. A conversation with Prof. Dr. Gerald Hüther. *Televizion*, *25*, 14–15.

Kagermann, H., Wahlster, W. & Helbig, J. (2013). *Securing the Future of German Manufacturing Industry: Recommendations for Implementing the Strategic Initiative INDUSTRIE 4.0, Final Report of the Industrie 4.0 Working Group*. Berlin, Germany: Forschungsunion im Stifterverband für die Deutsche Wirtschaft e.V.

Morin, E. (1992). From the Concept of System to the Paradigm of Complexity. *Journal of Social and Evolutionary Systems*, *15*(4), 371–385. doi:10.1016/1061-7361(92)90024-8

Pangaro, P. (1989). *The Architecture of Conversation Theory*. Retrieved from http://www.pangaro.com/L1L0/ArchCTBriefly2b.htm

Pask, G. (1975). *Conversation, Cognition and Learning: A Cybernetic Theory and Methodology*. New York, NY: Elsevier Publishing Company.

Varela, F. J., Thompson, E., & Rosch, E. (1993). *The Embodied Mind: Cognitive Science and Human Experience*. Cambridge, MA: The MIT Press.

Wilber, K. (2007). *The Integral Vision: A Very Short Introduction to the Revolutionary Integral Approach to Life, God, the Universe, and Everything*. Boston, MA: Shambhala Publications.

Related Readings

To continue IGI Global's long-standing tradition of advancing innovation through emerging research, please find below a compiled list of recommended IGI Global book chapters and journal articles in the areas of human-computer interaction, artificial intelligence, and smart environments. These related readings will provide additional information and guidance to further enrich your knowledge and assist you with your own research.

Abdulrahman, M. D., Subramanian, N., Chan, H. K., & Ning, K. (2017). Big Data Analytics: Academic Perspectives. In H. Chan, N. Subramanian, & M. Abdulrahman (Eds.), *Supply Chain Management in the Big Data Era* (pp. 1–12). Hershey, PA: IGI Global. doi:10.4018/978-1-5225-0956-1.ch001

Al-Aiad, A., Alkhatib, K., Al-Ayyad, M., & Hmeidi, I. (2016). A Conceptual Framework of Smart Home Context: An Empirical Investigation. *International Journal of Healthcare Information Systems and Informatics, 11*(3), 42–56. doi:10.4018/IJHISI.2016070103

Almajano, P., Lopez-Sanchez, M., Rodriguez, I., Puig, A., Llorente, M. S., & Ribera, M. (2016). Training Infrastructure to Participate in Real Life Institutions: Learning through Virtual Worlds. In F. Neto, R. de Souza, & A. Gomes (Eds.), *Handbook of Research on 3-D Virtual Environments and Hypermedia for Ubiquitous Learning* (pp. 192–219). Hershey, PA: IGI Global. doi:10.4018/978-1-5225-0125-1.ch008

Ammari, H. M., Shaout, A., & Mustapha, F. (2017). Sensing Coverage in Three-Dimensional Space: A Survey. In N. Ray & A. Turuk (Eds.), *Handbook of Research on Advanced Wireless Sensor Network Applications, Protocols, and Architectures* (pp. 1–28). Hershey, PA: IGI Global. doi:10.4018/978-1-5225-0486-3.ch001

Ang, L., Seng, K. P., & Heng, T. Z. (2016). Information Communication Assistive Technologies for Visually Impaired People. *International Journal of Ambient Computing and Intelligence*, *7*(1), 45–68. doi:10.4018/IJACI.2016010103

Ang, R. P., Tan, J. L., Goh, D. H., Huan, V. S., Ooi, Y. P., Boon, J. S., & Fung, D. S. (2017). A Game-Based Approach to Teaching Social Problem-Solving Skills. In R. Zheng & M. Gardner (Eds.), *Handbook of Research on Serious Games for Educational Applications* (pp. 168–195). Hershey, PA: IGI Global. doi:10.4018/978-1-5225-0513-6.ch008

Anthopoulos, L., Janssen, M., & Weerakkody, V. (2016). A Unified Smart City Model (USCM) for Smart City Conceptualization and Benchmarking. *International Journal of Electronic Government Research*, *12*(2), 77–93. doi:10.4018/IJEGR.2016040105

Antonova, A. (2017). Preparing for the Forthcoming Industrial Revolution: Beyond Virtual Worlds Technologies for Competence Development and Learning. *International Journal of Virtual and Augmented Reality*, *1*(1), 16–28. doi:10.4018/IJVAR.2017010102

Applin, S. A., & Fischer, M. D. (2017). Thing Theory: Connecting Humans to Smart Healthcare. In C. Reis & M. Maximiano (Eds.), *Internet of Things and Advanced Application in Healthcare* (pp. 249–265). Hershey, PA: IGI Global. doi:10.4018/978-1-5225-1820-4.ch009

Armstrong, S., & Yampolskiy, R. V. (2017). Security Solutions for Intelligent and Complex Systems. In M. Dawson, M. Eltayeb, & M. Omar (Eds.), *Security Solutions for Hyperconnectivity and the Internet of Things* (pp. 37–88). Hershey, PA: IGI Global. doi:10.4018/978-1-5225-0741-3.ch003

Auza, J. M., & de Marca, J. R. (2017). A Mobility Model for Crowd Sensing Simulation. *International Journal of Interdisciplinary Telecommunications and Networking*, *9*(1), 14–25. doi:10.4018/IJITN.2017010102

Ayesh, A., Arevalillo-Herráez, M., & Ferri, F. J. (2016). Towards Psychologically based Personalised Modelling of Emotions Using Associative Classifiers. *International Journal of Cognitive Informatics and Natural Intelligence*, *10*(2), 52–64. doi:10.4018/IJCINI.2016040103

Badilla, G. L., & Gaynor, J. M. (2017). Analysis of New Opotoelectronic Device for Detection of Heavy Metals in Corroded Soils: Design a Novel Optoelectronic Devices. In O. Sergiyenko & J. Rodriguez-Quiñonez (Eds.), *Developing and Applying Optoelectronics in Machine Vision* (pp. 273–302). Hershey, PA: IGI Global. doi:10.4018/978-1-5225-0632-4.ch009

Balas, C. E. (2016). An Artificial Neural Network Model as the Decision Support System of Ports. In E. Ocalir-Akunal (Ed.), *Using Decision Support Systems for Transportation Planning Efficiency* (pp. 36–60). Hershey, PA: IGI Global. doi:10.4018/978-1-4666-8648-9.ch002

Barbeito, A., Painho, M., Cabral, P., & ONeill, J. G. (2017). Beyond Digital Human Body Atlases: Segmenting an Integrated 3D Topological Model of the Human Body. *International Journal of E-Health and Medical Communications, 8*(1), 19–36. doi:10.4018/IJEHMC.2017010102

Berrahal, S., & Boudriga, N. (2017). The Risks of Wearable Technologies to Individuals and Organizations. In A. Marrington, D. Kerr, & J. Gammack (Eds.), *Managing Security Issues and the Hidden Dangers of Wearable Technologies* (pp. 18–46). Hershey, PA: IGI Global. doi:10.4018/978-1-5225-1016-1.ch002

Bhargavi, P., Jyothi, S., & Mamatha, D. M. (2017). A Study on Hybridization of Intelligent Techniques in Bioinformatics. In S. Bhattacharyya, S. De, I. Pan, & P. Dutta (Eds.), *Intelligent Multidimensional Data Clustering and Analysis* (pp. 358–379). Hershey, PA: IGI Global. doi:10.4018/978-1-5225-1776-4.ch014

Bhattacharya, S. (2017). A Predictive Linear Regression Model for Affective State Detection of Mobile Touch Screen Users. *International Journal of Mobile Human Computer Interaction, 9*(1), 30–44. doi:10.4018/IJMHCI.2017010103

Biagi, L., Comai, S., Mangiarotti, R., Matteucci, M., Negretti, M., & Yavuz, S. U. (2017). Enriching Geographic Maps with Accessible Paths Derived from Implicit Mobile Device Data Collection. In S. Konomi & G. Roussos (Eds.), *Enriching Urban Spaces with Ambient Computing, the Internet of Things, and Smart City Design* (pp. 89–113). Hershey, PA: IGI Global. doi:10.4018/978-1-5225-0827-4.ch005

Bogatinov, D. S., Bogdanoski, M., & Angelevski, S. (2016). AI-Based Cyber Defense for More Secure Cyberspace. In M. Hadji-Janev & M. Bogdanoski (Eds.), *Handbook of Research on Civil Society and National Security in the Era of Cyber Warfare* (pp. 220–237). Hershey, PA: IGI Global. doi:10.4018/978-1-4666-8793-6.ch011

Bottrighi, A., Leonardi, G., Piovesan, L., & Terenziani, P. (2016). Knowledge-Based Support to the Treatment of Exceptions in Computer Interpretable Clinical Guidelines. *International Journal of Knowledge-Based Organizations*, *6*(3), 1–27. doi:10.4018/IJKBO.2016070101

Bureš, V., Tučník, P., Mikulecký, P., Mls, K., & Blecha, P. (2016). Application of Ambient Intelligence in Educational Institutions: Visions and Architectures. *International Journal of Ambient Computing and Intelligence*, *7*(1), 94–120. doi:10.4018/IJACI.2016010105

Castellet, A. (2016). What If Devices Take Command: Content Innovation Perspectives for Smart Wearables in the Mobile Ecosystem. *International Journal of Handheld Computing Research*, *7*(2), 16–33. doi:10.4018/IJHCR.2016040102

Champaty, B., Ray, S. S., Mohapatra, B., & Pal, K. (2017). Voluntary Blink Controlled Communication Protocol for Bed-Ridden Patients. In N. Kamila (Ed.), *Handbook of Research on Wireless Sensor Network Trends, Technologies, and Applications* (pp. 162–195). Hershey, PA: IGI Global. doi:10.4018/978-1-5225-0501-3.ch008

Chawla, S. (2017). Multi-Agent-Based Information Retrieval System Using Information Scent in Query Log Mining for Effective Web Search. In G. Sreedhar (Ed.), *Web Data Mining and the Development of Knowledge-Based Decision Support Systems* (pp. 131–156). Hershey, PA: IGI Global. doi:10.4018/978-1-5225-1877-8.ch008

Chen, G., Wang, E., Sun, X., & Lu, Y. (2016). An Intelligent Approval System for City Construction based on Cloud Computing and Big Data. *International Journal of Grid and High Performance Computing*, *8*(3), 57–69. doi:10.4018/IJGHPC.2016070104

Cointault, F., Han, S., Rabatel, G., Jay, S., Rousseau, D., Billiot, B., & Salon, C. et al. (2017). 3D Imaging Systems for Agricultural Applications: Characterization of Crop and Root Phenotyping. In O. Sergiyenko & J. Rodriguez-Quiñonez (Eds.), *Developing and Applying Optoelectronics in Machine Vision* (pp. 236–272). Hershey, PA: IGI Global. doi:10.4018/978-1-5225-0632-4.ch008

Connor, A. M. (2016). A Historical Review of Creative Technologies. In A. Connor & S. Marks (Eds.), *Creative Technologies for Multidisciplinary Applications* (pp. 1–24). Hershey, PA: IGI Global. doi:10.4018/978-1-5225-0016-2.ch001

Connor, A. M., Sosa, R., Karmokar, S., Marks, S., Buxton, M., Gribble, A. M., & Foottit, J. et al. (2016). Exposing Core Competencies for Future Creative Technologists. In A. Connor & S. Marks (Eds.), *Creative Technologies for Multidisciplinary Applications* (pp. 377–397). Hershey, PA: IGI Global. doi:10.4018/978-1-5225-0016-2.ch015

Cook, A. E., & Wei, W. (2017). Using Eye Movements to Study Reading Processes: Methodological Considerations. In C. Was, F. Sansosti, & B. Morris (Eds.), *Eye-Tracking Technology Applications in Educational Research* (pp. 27–47). Hershey, PA: IGI Global. doi:10.4018/978-1-5225-1005-5.ch002

Corradini, A., & Mehta, M. (2016). A Graphical Tool for the Creation of Behaviors in Virtual Worlds. In J. Turner, M. Nixon, U. Bernardet, & S. DiPaola (Eds.), *Integrating Cognitive Architectures into Virtual Character Design* (pp. 65–93). Hershey, PA: IGI Global. doi:10.4018/978-1-5225-0454-2.ch003

Corrêa, L. D., & Dorn, M. (2017). Multi-Agent Systems in Three-Dimensional Protein Structure Prediction. In D. Adamatti (Ed.), *Multi-Agent-Based Simulations Applied to Biological and Environmental Systems* (pp. 241–278). Hershey, PA: IGI Global. doi:10.4018/978-1-5225-1756-6.ch011

Croatti, A., Ricci, A., & Viroli, M. (2017). Towards a Mobile Augmented Reality System for Emergency Management: The Case of SAFE. *International Journal of Distributed Systems and Technologies*, 8(1), 46–58. doi:10.4018/IJDST.2017010104

Dafer, M., & El-Abed, M. (2017). Evaluation of Keystroke Dynamics Authentication Systems: Analysis of Physical and Touch Screen Keyboards. In M. Dawson, D. Kisku, P. Gupta, J. Sing, & W. Li (Eds.), *Developing Next-Generation Countermeasures for Homeland Security Threat Prevention* (pp. 306–329). Hershey, PA: IGI Global. doi:10.4018/978-1-5225-0703-1.ch014

Das, P. K., Ghosh, D., Jagtap, P., Joshi, A., & Finin, T. (2017). Preserving User Privacy and Security in Context-Aware Mobile Platforms. In S. Mukherjea (Ed.), *Mobile Application Development, Usability, and Security* (pp. 166–193). Hershey, PA: IGI Global. doi:10.4018/978-1-5225-0945-5.ch008

De Filippi, F., Coscia, C., & Guido, R. (2017). How Technologies Can Enhance Open Policy Making and Citizen-Responsive Urban Planning: MiraMap - A Governing Tool for the Mirafiori Sud District in Turin (Italy). *International Journal of E-Planning Research, 6*(1), 23–42. doi:10.4018/IJEPR.2017010102

De Pasquale, D., Wood, E., Gottardo, A., Jones, J. A., Kaplan, R., & De-Marco, A. (2017). Tracking Children's Interactions with Traditional Text and Computer-Based Early Literacy Media. In C. Was, F. Sansosti, & B. Morris (Eds.), *Eye-Tracking Technology Applications in Educational Research* (pp. 107–121). Hershey, PA: IGI Global. doi:10.4018/978-1-5225-1005-5.ch006

Del Fiore, G., Mainetti, L., Mighali, V., Patrono, L., Alletto, S., Cucchiara, R., & Serra, G. (2016). A Location-Aware Architecture for an IoT-Based Smart Museum. *International Journal of Electronic Government Research, 12*(2), 39–55. doi:10.4018/IJEGR.2016040103

Desjarlais, M. (2017). The Use of Eye-gaze to Understand Multimedia Learning. In C. Was, F. Sansosti, & B. Morris (Eds.), *Eye-Tracking Technology Applications in Educational Research* (pp. 122–142). Hershey, PA: IGI Global. doi:10.4018/978-1-5225-1005-5.ch007

Diviacco, P., & Leadbetter, A. (2017). Balancing Formalization and Representation in Cross-Domain Data Management for Sustainable Development. In P. Diviacco, A. Leadbetter, & H. Glaves (Eds.), *Oceanographic and Marine Cross-Domain Data Management for Sustainable Development* (pp. 23–46). Hershey, PA: IGI Global. doi:10.4018/978-1-5225-0700-0.ch002

Dragoicea, M., Falcao e Cunha, J., Alexandru, M. V., & Constantinescu, D. A. (2017). Modelling and Simulation Perspective in Service Design: Experience in Transport Information Service Development. In S. Rozenes & Y. Cohen (Eds.), *Handbook of Research on Strategic Alliances and Value Co-Creation in the Service Industry* (pp. 374–399). Hershey, PA: IGI Global. doi:10.4018/978-1-5225-2084-9.ch019

El Khayat, G. A., & Fashal, N. A. (2017). Inter and Intra Cities Smartness: A Survey on Location Problems and GIS Tools. In S. Faiz & K. Mahmoudi (Eds.), *Handbook of Research on Geographic Information Systems Applications and Advancements* (pp. 296–320). Hershey, PA: IGI Global. doi:10.4018/978-1-5225-0937-0.ch011

Eteme, A. A., & Ngossaha, J. M. (2017). Urban Master Data Management: Case of the YUSIIP Platform. In S. Faiz & K. Mahmoudi (Eds.), *Handbook of Research on Geographic Information Systems Applications and Advancements* (pp. 441–465). Hershey, PA: IGI Global. doi:10.4018/978-1-5225-0937-0.ch018

Fisher, K. J., Nichols, T., Isbister, K., & Fuller, T. (2017). Quantifying "Magic": Creating Good Player Experiences on Xbox Kinect. In B. Dubbels (Ed.), *Transforming Gaming and Computer Simulation Technologies across Industries* (pp. 1–16). Hershey, PA: IGI Global. doi:10.4018/978-1-5225-1817-4.ch001

Flores-Fuentes, W., Rivas-Lopez, M., Hernandez-Balbuena, D., Sergiyenko, O., Rodríguez-Quiñonez, J. C., Rivera-Castillo, J., & Basaca-Preciado, L. C. et al. (2017). Applying Optoelectronic Devices Fusion in Machine Vision: Spatial Coordinate Measurement. In O. Sergiyenko & J. Rodriguez-Quiñonez (Eds.), *Developing and Applying Optoelectronics in Machine Vision* (pp. 1–37). Hershey, PA: IGI Global. doi:10.4018/978-1-5225-0632-4.ch001

Forti, I. (2017). A Cross Reading of Landscape through Digital Landscape Models: The Case of Southern Garda. In A. Ippolito (Ed.), *Handbook of Research on Emerging Technologies for Architectural and Archaeological Heritage* (pp. 532–561). Hershey, PA: IGI Global. doi:10.4018/978-1-5225-0675-1.ch018

Gammack, J., & Marrington, A. (2017). The Promise and Perils of Wearable Technologies. In A. Marrington, D. Kerr, & J. Gammack (Eds.), *Managing Security Issues and the Hidden Dangers of Wearable Technologies* (pp. 1–17). Hershey, PA: IGI Global. doi:10.4018/978-1-5225-1016-1.ch001

Ghaffarianhoseini, A., Ghaffarianhoseini, A., Tookey, J., Omrany, H., Fleury, A., Naismith, N., & Ghaffarianhoseini, M. (2016). The Essence of Smart Homes: Application of Intelligent Technologies towards Smarter Urban Future. In A. Connor & S. Marks (Eds.), *Creative Technologies for Multidisciplinary Applications* (pp. 334–376). Hershey, PA: IGI Global. doi:10.4018/978-1-5225-0016-2.ch014

Gharbi, A., De Runz, C., & Akdag, H. (2017). Urban Development Modelling: A Survey. In S. Faiz & K. Mahmoudi (Eds.), *Handbook of Research on Geographic Information Systems Applications and Advancements* (pp. 96–124). Hershey, PA: IGI Global. doi:10.4018/978-1-5225-0937-0.ch004

Ghosh, S., Mitra, S., Ghosh, S., & Chakraborty, S. (2017). Seismic Reliability Analysis in the Framework of Metamodelling Based Monte Carlo Simulation. In P. Samui, S. Chakraborty, & D. Kim (Eds.), *Modeling and Simulation Techniques in Structural Engineering* (pp. 192–208). Hershey, PA: IGI Global. doi:10.4018/978-1-5225-0588-4.ch006

Guesgen, H. W., & Marsland, S. (2016). Using Contextual Information for Recognising Human Behaviour. *International Journal of Ambient Computing and Intelligence*, 7(1), 27–44. doi:10.4018/IJACI.2016010102

Hameur Laine, A., & Brahimi, S. (2017). Background on Context-Aware Computing Systems. In C. Reis & M. Maximiano (Eds.), *Internet of Things and Advanced Application in Healthcare* (pp. 1–31). Hershey, PA: IGI Global. doi:10.4018/978-1-5225-1820-4.ch001

Harrati, N., Bouchrika, I., Mahfouf, Z., & Ladjailia, A. (2017). Evaluation Methods for E-Learning Applications in Terms of User Satisfaction and Interface Usability. In P. Vu, S. Fredrickson, & C. Moore (Eds.), *Handbook of Research on Innovative Pedagogies and Technologies for Online Learning in Higher Education* (pp. 427–448). Hershey, PA: IGI Global. doi:10.4018/978-1-5225-1851-8.ch018

Harwood, T. (2016). Machinima: A Meme of Our Time. In A. Connor & S. Marks (Eds.), *Creative Technologies for Multidisciplinary Applications* (pp. 149–181). Hershey, PA: IGI Global. doi:10.4018/978-1-5225-0016-2.ch007

Hassani, K., & Lee, W. (2016). A Universal Architecture for Migrating Cognitive Agents: A Case Study on Automatic Animation Generation. In J. Turner, M. Nixon, U. Bernardet, & S. DiPaola (Eds.), *Integrating Cognitive Architectures into Virtual Character Design* (pp. 238–265). Hershey, PA: IGI Global. doi:10.4018/978-1-5225-0454-2.ch009

Herpich, F., Nunes, F. B., Voss, G. B., & Medina, R. D. (2016). Three-Dimensional Virtual Environment and NPC: A Perspective about Intelligent Agents Ubiquitous. In F. Neto, R. de Souza, & A. Gomes (Eds.), *Handbook of Research on 3-D Virtual Environments and Hypermedia for Ubiquitous Learning* (pp. 510–536). Hershey, PA: IGI Global. doi:10.4018/978-1-5225-0125-1.ch021

Higgins, C., Kearns, Á., Ryan, C., & Fernstrom, M. (2016). The Role of Gamification and Evolutionary Computation in the Provision of Self-Guided Speech Therapy. In D. Novák, B. Tulu, & H. Brendryen (Eds.), *Handbook of Research on Holistic Perspectives in Gamification for Clinical Practice* (pp. 158–182). Hershey, PA: IGI Global. doi:10.4018/978-1-4666-9522-1.ch008

Honarvar, A. R., & Sami, A. (2016). Extracting Usage Patterns from Power Usage Data of Homes Appliances in Smart Home using Big Data Platform. *International Journal of Information Technology and Web Engineering*, *11*(2), 39–50. doi:10.4018/IJITWE.2016040103

Hulsey, N. (2016). Between Games and Simulation: Gamification and Convergence in Creative Computing. In A. Connor & S. Marks (Eds.), *Creative Technologies for Multidisciplinary Applications* (pp. 130–148). Hershey, PA: IGI Global. doi:10.4018/978-1-5225-0016-2.ch006

Ion, A., & Patrascu, M. (2017). Agent Based Modelling of Smart Structures: The Challenges of a New Research Domain. In P. Samui, S. Chakraborty, & D. Kim (Eds.), *Modeling and Simulation Techniques in Structural Engineering* (pp. 38–60). Hershey, PA: IGI Global. doi:10.4018/978-1-5225-0588-4.ch002

Iyawe, B. I. (2017). User Performance Testing Indicator: User Performance Indicator Tool (UPIT). In S. Saeed, Y. Bamarouf, T. Ramayah, & S. Iqbal (Eds.), *Design Solutions for User-Centric Information Systems* (pp. 205–229). Hershey, PA: IGI Global. doi:10.4018/978-1-5225-1944-7.ch012

Izumi, S., Hata, M., Takahira, H., Soylu, M., Edo, A., Abe, T., & Suganuma, T. (2017). A Proposal of SDN Based Disaster-Aware Smart Routing for Highly-Available Information Storage Systems and Its Evaluation. *International Journal of Software Science and Computational Intelligence*, *9*(1), 68–82. doi:10.4018/IJSSCI.2017010105

Jarušek, R., & Kocian, V. (2017). Artificial Intelligence Algorithms for Classification and Pattern Recognition. In E. Volna, M. Kotyrba, & M. Janosek (Eds.), *Pattern Recognition and Classification in Time Series Data* (pp. 53–85). Hershey, PA: IGI Global. doi:10.4018/978-1-5225-0565-5.ch003

Jayabalan, J., Yildirim, D., Kim, D., & Samui, P. (2017). Design Optimization of a Wind Turbine Using Artificial Intelligence. In M. Ram & J. Davim (Eds.), *Mathematical Concepts and Applications in Mechanical Engineering and Mechatronics* (pp. 38–66). Hershey, PA: IGI Global. doi:10.4018/978-1-5225-1639-2.ch003

Jena, G. C. (2017). Multi-Sensor Data Fusion (MSDF). In N. Ray & A. Turuk (Eds.), *Handbook of Research on Advanced Wireless Sensor Network Applications, Protocols, and Architectures* (pp. 29–61). Hershey, PA: IGI Global. doi:10.4018/978-1-5225-0486-3.ch002

Kale, G. V., & Patil, V. H. (2016). A Study of Vision based Human Motion Recognition and Analysis. *International Journal of Ambient Computing and Intelligence*, *7*(2), 75–92. doi:10.4018/IJACI.2016070104

Kasemsap, K. (2017). Mastering Intelligent Decision Support Systems in Enterprise Information Management. In G. Sreedhar (Ed.), *Web Data Mining and the Development of Knowledge-Based Decision Support Systems* (pp. 35–56). Hershey, PA: IGI Global. doi:10.4018/978-1-5225-1877-8.ch004

Kim, S. (2017). New Game Paradigm for IoT Systems. In *Game Theory Solutions for the Internet of Things: Emerging Research and Opportunities* (pp. 101–147). Hershey, PA: IGI Global. doi:10.4018/978-1-5225-1952-2.ch004

Related Readings

Ladjailia, A., Bouchrika, I., Harrati, N., & Mahfouf, Z. (2017). Encoding Human Motion for Automated Activity Recognition in Surveillance Applications. In N. Dey, A. Ashour, & S. Acharjee (Eds.), *Applied Video Processing in Surveillance and Monitoring Systems* (pp. 170–192). Hershey, PA: IGI Global. doi:10.4018/978-1-5225-1022-2.ch008

Lanza, J., Sotres, P., Sánchez, L., Galache, J. A., Santana, J. R., Gutiérrez, V., & Muñoz, L. (2016). Managing Large Amounts of Data Generated by a Smart City Internet of Things Deployment. *International Journal on Semantic Web and Information Systems*, *12*(4), 22–42. doi:10.4018/IJSWIS.2016100102

Lee, H. (2017). The Internet of Things and Assistive Technologies for People with Disabilities: Applications, Trends, and Issues. In C. Reis & M. Maximiano (Eds.), *Internet of Things and Advanced Application in Healthcare* (pp. 32–65). Hershey, PA: IGI Global. doi:10.4018/978-1-5225-1820-4.ch002

Li, W. H., Zhu, K., & Fu, H. (2017). Exploring the Design Space of Bezel-Initiated Gestures for Mobile Interaction. *International Journal of Mobile Human Computer Interaction*, *9*(1), 16–29. doi:10.4018/IJMHCI.2017010102

Ludwig, T., Kotthaus, C., & Pipek, V. (2015). Should I Try Turning It Off and On Again?: Outlining HCI Challenges for Cyber-Physical Production Systems. *International Journal of Information Systems for Crisis Response and Management*, *7*(3), 55–68. doi:10.4018/ijiscram.2015070104

Luo, L., Kiewra, K. A., Peteranetz, M. S., & Flanigan, A. E. (2017). Using Eye-Tracking Technology to Understand How Graphic Organizers Aid Student Learning. In C. Was, F. Sansosti, & B. Morris (Eds.), *Eye-Tracking Technology Applications in Educational Research* (pp. 220–238). Hershey, PA: IGI Global. doi:10.4018/978-1-5225-1005-5.ch011

Mahanty, R., & Mahanti, P. K. (2016). Unleashing Artificial Intelligence onto Big Data: A Review. In S. Dash & B. Subudhi (Eds.), *Handbook of Research on Computational Intelligence Applications in Bioinformatics* (pp. 1–16). Hershey, PA: IGI Global. doi:10.4018/978-1-5225-0427-6.ch001

Marzuki, A. (2017). CMOS Image Sensor: Analog and Mixed-Signal Circuits. In O. Sergiyenko & J. Rodriguez-Quiñonez (Eds.), *Developing and Applying Optoelectronics in Machine Vision* (pp. 38–78). Hershey, PA: IGI Global. doi:10.4018/978-1-5225-0632-4.ch002

McKenna, H. P. (2017). Urbanizing the Ambient: Why People Matter So Much in Smart Cities. In S. Konomi & G. Roussos (Eds.), *Enriching Urban Spaces with Ambient Computing, the Internet of Things, and Smart City Design* (pp. 209–231). Hershey, PA: IGI Global. doi:10.4018/978-1-5225-0827-4.ch011

Meghanathan, N. (2017). Diameter-Aggregation Delay Tradeoff for Data Gathering Trees in Wireless Sensor Networks. In N. Kamila (Ed.), *Handbook of Research on Wireless Sensor Network Trends, Technologies, and Applications* (pp. 237–253). Hershey, PA: IGI Global. doi:10.4018/978-1-5225-0501-3.ch010

Moein, S. (2014). Artificial Intelligence in Medical Science. In *Medical Diagnosis Using Artificial Neural Networks* (pp. 11–23). Hershey, PA: IGI Global. doi:10.4018/978-1-4666-6146-2.ch002

Moein, S. (2014). Artificial Neural Network for Medical Diagnosis. In *Medical Diagnosis Using Artificial Neural Networks* (pp. 85–94). Hershey, PA: IGI Global. doi:10.4018/978-1-4666-6146-2.ch007

Moein, S. (2014). Types of Artificial Neural Network. In *Medical Diagnosis Using Artificial Neural Networks* (pp. 58–67). Hershey, PA: IGI Global. doi:10.4018/978-1-4666-6146-2.ch005

Moser, S. (2017). Linking Virtual and Real-life Environments: Scrutinizing Ubiquitous Learning Scenarios. In S. Şad & M. Ebner (Eds.), *Digital Tools for Seamless Learning* (pp. 214–239). Hershey, PA: IGI Global. doi:10.4018/978-1-5225-1692-7.ch011

Mumini, O. O., Adebisi, F. M., Edward, O. O., & Abidemi, A. S. (2016). Simulation of Stock Prediction System using Artificial Neural Networks. *International Journal of Business Analytics*, *3*(3), 25–44. doi:10.4018/IJBAN.2016070102

Muñoz, M. C., & Moh, M. (2017). Authentication of Smart Grid: The Case for Using Merkle Trees. In M. Ferrag & A. Ahmim (Eds.), *Security Solutions and Applied Cryptography in Smart Grid Communications* (pp. 117–136). Hershey, PA: IGI Global. doi:10.4018/978-1-5225-1829-7.ch007

Mushcab, H., Kernohan, W. G., Wallace, J., Harper, R., & Martin, S. (2017). Self-Management of Diabetes Mellitus with Remote Monitoring: A Retrospective Review of 214 Cases. *International Journal of E-Health and Medical Communications*, 8(1), 52–61. doi:10.4018/IJEHMC.2017010104

Mutlu-Bayraktar, D. (2017). Usability Evaluation of Social Media Web Sites and Applications via Eye-Tracking Method. In S. Hai-Jew (Ed.), *Social Media Data Extraction and Content Analysis* (pp. 85–112). Hershey, PA: IGI Global. doi:10.4018/978-1-5225-0648-5.ch004

Nadler, S. (2017). Mobile Location Tracking: Indoor and Outdoor Location Tracking. In S. Mukherjea (Ed.), *Mobile Application Development, Usability, and Security* (pp. 194–209). Hershey, PA: IGI Global. doi:10.4018/978-1-5225-0945-5.ch009

Nagpal, R., Mehrotra, D., & Bhatia, P. K. (2017). The State of Art in Website Usability Evaluation Methods. In S. Saeed, Y. Bamarouf, T. Ramayah, & S. Iqbal (Eds.), *Design Solutions for User-Centric Information Systems* (pp. 275–296). Hershey, PA: IGI Global. doi:10.4018/978-1-5225-1944-7.ch015

Nava, J., & Osorio, A. (2016). A Hybrid Intelligent Risk Identification Model for Configuration Management in Aerospace Systems. In A. Ochoa-Zezzatti, J. Sánchez, M. Cedillo-Campos, & M. de Lourdes (Eds.), *Handbook of Research on Military, Aeronautical, and Maritime Logistics and Operations* (pp. 319–345). Hershey, PA: IGI Global. doi:10.4018/978-1-4666-9779-9.ch017

Nazareth, A., Odean, R., & Pruden, S. M. (2017). The Use of Eye-Tracking in Spatial Thinking Research. In C. Was, F. Sansosti, & B. Morris (Eds.), *Eye-Tracking Technology Applications in Educational Research* (pp. 239–260). Hershey, PA: IGI Global. doi:10.4018/978-1-5225-1005-5.ch012

Neves, J., Zeleznikow, J., & Vicente, H. (2016). Quality of Judgment Assessment. In P. Novais & D. Carneiro (Eds.), *Interdisciplinary Perspectives on Contemporary Conflict Resolution* (pp. 96–110). Hershey, PA: IGI Global. doi:10.4018/978-1-5225-0245-6.ch006

Niewiadomski, R., & Anderson, D. (2017). The Rise of Artificial Intelligence: Its Impact on Labor Market and Beyond. In R. Batko & A. Szopa (Eds.), *Strategic Imperatives and Core Competencies in the Era of Robotics and Artificial Intelligence* (pp. 29–49). Hershey, PA: IGI Global. doi:10.4018/978-1-5225-1656-9.ch003

Nishani, L., & Biba, M. (2017). Statistical Relational Learning for Collaborative Filtering a State-of-the-Art Review. In V. Bhatnagar (Ed.), *Collaborative Filtering Using Data Mining and Analysis* (pp. 250–269). Hershey, PA: IGI Global. doi:10.4018/978-1-5225-0489-4.ch014

Ogata, T. (2016). Computational and Cognitive Approaches to Narratology from the Perspective of Narrative Generation. In T. Ogata & T. Akimoto (Eds.), *Computational and Cognitive Approaches to Narratology* (pp. 1–74). Hershey, PA: IGI Global. doi:10.4018/978-1-5225-0432-0.ch001

Ozpinar, A., & Kucukasci, E. S. (2016). Use of Chaotic Randomness Numbers: Metaheuristic and Artificial Intelligence Algorithms. In N. Celebi (Ed.), *Intelligent Techniques for Data Analysis in Diverse Settings* (pp. 207–227). Hershey, PA: IGI Global. doi:10.4018/978-1-5225-0075-9.ch010

Ozpinar, A., & Ozil, E. (2016). Smart Grid and Demand Side Management: Application of Metaheuristic and Artificial Intelligence Algorithms. In A. Ahmad & N. Hassan (Eds.), *Smart Grid as a Solution for Renewable and Efficient Energy* (pp. 49–68). Hershey, PA: IGI Global. doi:10.4018/978-1-5225-0072-8.ch003

Papadopoulos, H. (2016). Designing Smart Home Environments for Unobtrusive Monitoring for Independent Living: The Use Case of USEFIL. *International Journal of E-Services and Mobile Applications*, 8(1), 47–63. doi:10.4018/IJESMA.2016010104

Papadopoulos, H. (2016). Modeling Place: Usage of Mobile Data Services and Applications within Different Places. *International Journal of E-Services and Mobile Applications*, 8(2), 1–20. doi:10.4018/IJESMA.2016040101

Parey, A., & Ahuja, A. S. (2016). Application of Artificial Intelligence to Gearbox Fault Diagnosis: A Review. In S. John (Ed.), *Handbook of Research on Generalized and Hybrid Set Structures and Applications for Soft Computing* (pp. 536–562). Hershey, PA: IGI Global. doi:10.4018/978-1-4666-9798-0.ch024

Parikh, C. (2017). Eye-Tracking Technology: A Closer Look at Eye-Tracking Paradigms with High-Risk Populations. In C. Was, F. Sansosti, & B. Morris (Eds.), *Eye-Tracking Technology Applications in Educational Research* (pp. 283–302). Hershey, PA: IGI Global. doi:10.4018/978-1-5225-1005-5.ch014

Peng, M., Qin, Y., Tang, C., & Deng, X. (2016). An E-Commerce Customer Service Robot Based on Intention Recognition Model. *Journal of Electronic Commerce in Organizations*, *14*(1), 34–44. doi:10.4018/JECO.2016010104

Pessoa, C. R., & Júnior, M. D. (2017). A Telecommunications Approach in Systems for Effective Logistics and Supply Chains. In G. Jamil, A. Soares, & C. Pessoa (Eds.), *Handbook of Research on Information Management for Effective Logistics and Supply Chains* (pp. 437–452). Hershey, PA: IGI Global. doi:10.4018/978-1-5225-0973-8.ch023

Pineda, R. G. (2016). Where the Interaction Is Not: Reflections on the Philosophy of Human-Computer Interaction. *International Journal of Art, Culture and Design Technologies*, *5*(1), 1–12. doi:10.4018/IJACDT.2016010101

Poitras, E. G., Harley, J. M., Compeau, T., Kee, K., & Lajoie, S. P. (2017). Augmented Reality in Informal Learning Settings: Leveraging Technology for the Love of History. In R. Zheng & M. Gardner (Eds.), *Handbook of Research on Serious Games for Educational Applications* (pp. 272–293). Hershey, PA: IGI Global. doi:10.4018/978-1-5225-0513-6.ch013

Powell, W. A., Corbett, N., & Powell, V. (2016). The Rise of the Virtual Human. In A. Connor & S. Marks (Eds.), *Creative Technologies for Multidisciplinary Applications* (pp. 99–129). Hershey, PA: IGI Global. doi:10.4018/978-1-5225-0016-2.ch005

Prakash, L. S., & Saini, D. K. (2017). Instructional Design Technology in Higher Education System: Role and Impact on Developing Creative Learning Environments. In C. Zhou (Ed.), *Handbook of Research on Creative Problem-Solving Skill Development in Higher Education* (pp. 378–406). Hershey, PA: IGI Global. doi:10.4018/978-1-5225-0643-0.ch017

Rahmani, M. E., Amine, A., & Hamou, R. M. (2016). Supervised Machine Learning for Plants Identification Based on Images of Their Leaves. *International Journal of Agricultural and Environmental Information Systems*, *7*(4), 17–31. doi:10.4018/IJAEIS.2016100102

Ramanathan, U. (2017). How Smart Operations Help Better Planning and Replenishment?: Empirical Study – Supply Chain Collaboration for Smart Operations. In H. Chan, N. Subramanian, & M. Abdulrahman (Eds.), *Supply Chain Management in the Big Data Era* (pp. 25–49). Hershey, PA: IGI Global. doi:10.4018/978-1-5225-0956-1.ch003

Rao, M., & Kamila, N. K. (2017). Target Tracking in Wireless Sensor Network: The Current State of Art. In N. Kamila (Ed.), *Handbook of Research on Wireless Sensor Network Trends, Technologies, and Applications* (pp. 413–437). Hershey, PA: IGI Global. doi:10.4018/978-1-5225-0501-3.ch017

Rappaport, J. M., Richter, S. B., & Kennedy, D. T. (2016). A Strategic Perspective on Using Symbolic Transformation in STEM Education: Robotics and Automation. *International Journal of Strategic Decision Sciences*, 7(1), 39–75. doi:10.4018/IJSDS.2016010103

Rashid, E. (2016). R4 Model for Case-Based Reasoning and Its Application for Software Fault Prediction. *International Journal of Software Science and Computational Intelligence*, 8(3), 19–38. doi:10.4018/IJSSCI.2016070102

Rathore, M. M., Paul, A., Ahmad, A., & Jeon, G. (2017). IoT-Based Big Data: From Smart City towards Next Generation Super City Planning. *International Journal on Semantic Web and Information Systems*, 13(1), 28–47. doi:10.4018/IJSWIS.2017010103

Reeberg de Mello, A., & Stemmer, M. R. (2017). Automated Visual Inspection System for Printed Circuit Boards for Small Series Production: A Multiagent Context Approach. In O. Sergiyenko & J. Rodriguez-Quiñonez (Eds.), *Developing and Applying Optoelectronics in Machine Vision* (pp. 79–107). Hershey, PA: IGI Global. doi:10.4018/978-1-5225-0632-4.ch003

Rodrigues, P., & Rosa, P. J. (2017). Eye-Tracking as a Research Methodology in Educational Context: A Spanning Framework. In C. Was, F. Sansosti, & B. Morris (Eds.), *Eye-Tracking Technology Applications in Educational Research* (pp. 1–26). Hershey, PA: IGI Global. doi:10.4018/978-1-5225-1005-5.ch001

Rosen, Y., & Mosharraf, M. (2016). Computer Agent Technologies in Collaborative Assessments. In Y. Rosen, S. Ferrara, & M. Mosharraf (Eds.), *Handbook of Research on Technology Tools for Real-World Skill Development* (pp. 319–343). Hershey, PA: IGI Global. doi:10.4018/978-1-4666-9441-5.ch012

Rosenzweig, E. D., & Bendoly, E. (2017). An Investigation of Competitor Networks in Manufacturing Strategy and Implications for Performance. In A. Vlachvei, O. Notta, K. Karantininis, & N. Tsounis (Eds.), *Factors Affecting Firm Competitiveness and Performance in the Modern Business World* (pp. 43–82). Hershey, PA: IGI Global. doi:10.4018/978-1-5225-0843-4.ch002

Saiz-Alvarez, J. M., & Leal, G. C. (2017). Cybersecurity Best Practices and Cultural Change in Global Business: Some Perspectives from the European Union. In G. Afolayan & A. Akinwale (Eds.), *Global Perspectives on Development Administration and Cultural Change* (pp. 48–73). Hershey, PA: IGI Global. doi:10.4018/978-1-5225-0629-4.ch003

Sang, Y., Zhu, Y., Zhao, H., & Tang, M. (2016). Study on an Interactive Truck Crane Simulation Platform Based on Virtual Reality Technology. *International Journal of Distance Education Technologies, 14*(2), 64–78. doi:10.4018/IJDET.2016040105

Sarkar, D., & Roy, J. K. (2016). Artificial Neural Network (ANN) in Network Reconfiguration for Improvement of Voltage Stability. In S. Shandilya, S. Shandilya, T. Thakur, & A. Nagar (Eds.), *Handbook of Research on Emerging Technologies for Electrical Power Planning, Analysis, and Optimization* (pp. 184–206). Hershey, PA: IGI Global. doi:10.4018/978-1-4666-9911-3.ch010

Schafer, S. B. (2016). The Media-Sphere as Dream: Researching the Contextual Unconscious of Collectives. In S. Schafer (Ed.), *Exploring the Collective Unconscious in the Age of Digital Media* (pp. 232–260). Hershey, PA: IGI Global. doi:10.4018/978-1-4666-9891-8.ch010

Scheiter, K., & Eitel, A. (2017). The Use of Eye Tracking as a Research and Instructional Tool in Multimedia Learning. In C. Was, F. Sansosti, & B. Morris (Eds.), *Eye-Tracking Technology Applications in Educational Research* (pp. 143–164). Hershey, PA: IGI Global. doi:10.4018/978-1-5225-1005-5.ch008

Schneegass, S., Olsson, T., Mayer, S., & van Laerhoven, K. (2016). Mobile Interactions Augmented by Wearable Computing: A Design Space and Vision. *International Journal of Mobile Human Computer Interaction, 8*(4), 104–114. doi:10.4018/IJMHCI.2016100106

Shah, Z., & Kolhe, A. (2017). Throughput Analysis of IEEE 802.11ac and IEEE 802.11n in a Residential Home Environment. *International Journal of Interdisciplinary Telecommunications and Networking, 9*(1), 1–13. doi:10.4018/IJITN.2017010101

Shaqrah, A. A. (2016). Future of Smart Cities in the Knowledge-based Urban Development and the Role of Award Competitions. *International Journal of Knowledge-Based Organizations*, 6(1), 49–59. doi:10.4018/IJKBO.2016010104

Shayan, S., Abrahamson, D., Bakker, A., Duijzer, C. A., & van der Schaaf, M. (2017). Eye-Tracking the Emergence of Attentional Anchors in a Mathematics Learning Tablet Activity. In C. Was, F. Sansosti, & B. Morris (Eds.), *Eye-Tracking Technology Applications in Educational Research* (pp. 166–194). Hershey, PA: IGI Global. doi:10.4018/978-1-5225-1005-5.ch009

Sosnin, P. I. (2017). Conceptual Experiments in Automated Designing. In R. Zuanon (Ed.), *Projective Processes and Neuroscience in Art and Design* (pp. 155–181). Hershey, PA: IGI Global. doi:10.4018/978-1-5225-0510-5.ch010

Starostenko, O., Cruz-Perez, C., Alarcon-Aquino, V., Melnik, V. I., & Tyrsa, V. (2017). Machine Vision Application on Science and Industry: Real-Time Face Sensing and Recognition in Machine Vision – Trends and New Advances. In O. Sergiyenko & J. Rodriguez-Quiñonez (Eds.), *Developing and Applying Optoelectronics in Machine Vision* (pp. 146–179). Hershey, PA: IGI Global. doi:10.4018/978-1-5225-0632-4.ch005

Stasolla, F., Boccasini, A., & Perilli, V. (2017). Assistive Technology-Based Programs to Support Adaptive Behaviors by Children with Autism Spectrum Disorders: A Literature Overview. In Y. Kats (Ed.), *Supporting the Education of Children with Autism Spectrum Disorders* (pp. 140–159). Hershey, PA: IGI Global. doi:10.4018/978-1-5225-0816-8.ch008

Stratigea, A., Leka, A., & Panagiotopoulou, M. (2017). In Search of Indicators for Assessing Smart and Sustainable Cities and Communities Performance. *International Journal of E-Planning Research*, 6(1), 43–73. doi:10.4018/IJEPR.2017010103

Su, S., Lin, H. K., Wang, C., & Huang, Z. (2016). Multi-Modal Affective Computing Technology Design the Interaction between Computers and Human of Intelligent Tutoring Systems. *International Journal of Online Pedagogy and Course Design*, 6(1), 13–28. doi:10.4018/IJOPCD.2016010102

Sun, X., May, A., & Wang, Q. (2017). Investigation of the Role of Mobile Personalisation at Large Sports Events. *International Journal of Mobile Human Computer Interaction*, 9(1), 1–15. doi:10.4018/IJMHCI.2017010101

Szopa, A. (2017). The Influence of Crowdsourcing Business Model into Artificial Intelligence. In R. Batko & A. Szopa (Eds.), *Strategic Imperatives and Core Competencies in the Era of Robotics and Artificial Intelligence* (pp. 15–28). Hershey, PA: IGI Global. doi:10.4018/978-1-5225-1656-9.ch002

Tokunaga, S., Tamamizu, K., Saiki, S., Nakamura, M., & Yasuda, K. (2017). VirtualCareGiver: Personalized Smart Elderly Care. *International Journal of Software Innovation*, 5(1), 30–43. doi:10.4018/IJSI.2017010103

Trabelsi, I., & Bouhlel, M. S. (2016). Comparison of Several Acoustic Modeling Techniques for Speech Emotion Recognition. *International Journal of Synthetic Emotions*, 7(1), 58–68. doi:10.4018/IJSE.2016010105

Truman, B. (2017). New Constructions for Understanding using Virtual Learning- Towards Transdisciplinarity. In A. Stricker, C. Calongne, B. Truman, & F. Arenas (Eds.), *Integrating an Awareness of Selfhood and Society into Virtual Learning* (pp. 316–334). Hershey, PA: IGI Global. doi:10.4018/978-1-5225-2182-2.ch019

Turner, J. O. (2016). Virtual Soar-Agent Implementations: Examples, Issues, and Speculations. In J. Turner, M. Nixon, U. Bernardet, & S. DiPaola (Eds.), *Integrating Cognitive Architectures into Virtual Character Design* (pp. 181–212). Hershey, PA: IGI Global. doi:10.4018/978-1-5225-0454-2.ch007

Urrea, C., & Uren, V. (2017). Technical Evaluation, Development, and Implementation of a Remote Monitoring System for a Golf Cart. In N. Dey, A. Ashour, & S. Acharjee (Eds.), *Applied Video Processing in Surveillance and Monitoring Systems* (pp. 220–243). Hershey, PA: IGI Global. doi:10.4018/978-1-5225-1022-2.ch010

Veerapathiran, N., & Anand, S. (2017). Reducing False Alarms in Vision-Based Fire Detection. In N. Dey, A. Ashour, & S. Acharjee (Eds.), *Applied Video Processing in Surveillance and Monitoring Systems* (pp. 263–290). Hershey, PA: IGI Global. doi:10.4018/978-1-5225-1022-2.ch012

Vorraber, W., Lichtenegger, G., Brugger, J., Gojmerac, I., Egly, M., Panzenböck, K., & Voessner, S. et al. (2016). Designing Information Systems to Facilitate Civil-Military Cooperation in Disaster Management. *International Journal of Distributed Systems and Technologies*, 7(4), 22–40. doi:10.4018/IJDST.2016100102

Vyas, D., Kröner, A., & Nijholt, A. (2016). From Mundane to Smart: Exploring Interactions with Smart Design Objects. *International Journal of Mobile Human Computer Interaction, 8*(1), 59–82. doi:10.4018/IJMHCI.2016010103

Wang, L., Li, C., & Wu, J. (2017). The Status of Research into Intention Recognition. In J. Wu (Ed.), *Improving the Quality of Life for Dementia Patients through Progressive Detection, Treatment, and Care* (pp. 201–221). Hershey, PA: IGI Global. doi:10.4018/978-1-5225-0925-7.ch010

Wang, Y., Valipour, M., & Zatarain, O. A. (2016). Quantitative Semantic Analysis and Comprehension by Cognitive Machine Learning. *International Journal of Cognitive Informatics and Natural Intelligence, 10*(3), 13–28. doi:10.4018/IJCINI.2016070102

Xie, L., Zheng, L., & Yang, G. (2017). Hybrid Integration Technology for Wearable Sensor Systems. In C. Reis & M. Maximiano (Eds.), *Internet of Things and Advanced Application in Healthcare* (pp. 98–137). Hershey, PA: IGI Global. doi:10.4018/978-1-5225-1820-4.ch004

Xing, B., & Gao, W. (2014). Overview of Computational Intelligence. In *Computational Intelligence in Remanufacturing* (pp. 18–36). Hershey, PA: IGI Global. doi:10.4018/978-1-4666-4908-8.ch002

Xu, R., Li, Z., Cui, P., Zhu, S., & Gao, A. (2016). A Geometric Dynamic Temporal Reasoning Method with Tags for Cognitive Systems. *International Journal of Software Science and Computational Intelligence, 8*(4), 43–59. doi:10.4018/IJSSCI.2016100103

Yamaguchi, T., Nishimura, T., & Takadama, K. (2016). Awareness Based Recommendation: Passively Interactive Learning System. *International Journal of Robotics Applications and Technologies, 4*(1), 83–99. doi:10.4018/IJRAT.2016010105

Zentall, S. R., & Junglen, A. G. (2017). Investigating Mindsets and Motivation through Eye Tracking and Other Physiological Measures. In C. Was, F. Sansosti, & B. Morris (Eds.), *Eye-Tracking Technology Applications in Educational Research* (pp. 48–64). Hershey, PA: IGI Global. doi:10.4018/978-1-5225-1005-5.ch003

Related Readings

Zielinska, T. (2016). Professional and Personal Service Robots. *International Journal of Robotics Applications and Technologies*, *4*(1), 63–82. doi:10.4018/IJRAT.2016010104

Zohora, S. E., Khan, A. M., Srivastava, A. K., Nguyen, N. G., & Dey, N. (2016). A Study of the State of the Art in Synthetic Emotional Intelligence in Affective Computing. *International Journal of Synthetic Emotions*, *7*(1), 1–12. doi:10.4018/IJSE.2016010101

About the Author

Benjamin Hadorn earned his PhD from the University of Fribourg, Switzerland, where he studied computer science, in particular coordination in the context of pervasive and mobile computing. He worked 15 years as a software architect and engineer, developing smart and intelligent industrial machines. In 2016 he founded a start-up company for human-centered and sustainable system engineering, called CyberTech Engineering GmbH.

Index

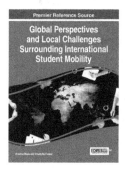
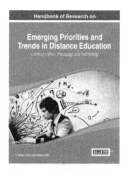
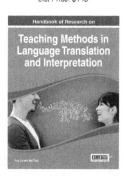

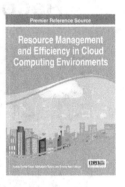

Printed in the United States
By Bookmasters